THE

LANKAVATARA

SUTRA

What I Teach is Tathagatahood in the sense of Dharmakaya, Ultimate Oneness, Nirvana, emptiness, unbornness, unqualifiedness, devoid of will-effort. The reason why I teach the doctrine of Tathagatahood is to cause the ignorant and simple-minded to lay aside their fears as they listen to the teaching of egolessness and come to understand the state of nondiscrimination and imagelessness.

Lankavatara Sutra

The Lankavatara Sutra

An Epitomized Version

Translated by D.T. Suzuki

Compiled and Edited by Dwight Goddard

Foreword by John Daido Loori

MONKFISH BOOK PUBLISHING COMPANY

RHINEBECK, NEW YORK

Provenance Editions
Volume 1

ISBN 0-9726357-4-2

Book and cover design by Georgia Dent
Front cover art by Marilyn Stablein

Bulk purchase discounts, for educational or promotional purposes, are
available. Contact the publisher for more information.

First edition

First impression

10 9 8 7 6 5 4 3 2 1

Provenance Editions is dedicated to reprints of classics of spiritual
literature in elegant and durable editions. Provenance Editions are
published by
Monkfish Book Publishing Company
27 Lamoree Road
Rhinebeck, NY 12572
www.monkfishpublishing.com

Table of Contents

Dedicated
TO MY HONORED TEACHERS

Daisetz Teitaro Suzuki
PROFESSOR, OTANI UNIVERSITY

Taiko Yamazaki
ROSHI, SO-KO-KU MONASTERY

Foreword to the Provenance Edition of The Lankavatara Sutra

THE *LANKAVATARA SUTRA* is one of the major texts of Mahayana Buddhism and one of a handful of sutras that are central to the study of Zen. It is said that the Indian monk Bodhidharma, the first ancestor of the Zen school, introduced the *Lankavatara Sutra* to China some time in the fifth century, and that he passed on its teachings — along with the robe and bowl of the transmission of the dharma — to his successor, Huiko.

Lankavatara Sutra is the Sanskrit title for the "Sutra on the Descent to Sri Lanka." The scene of the sutra is an assembly in Sri Lanka where the Buddha responds to questions presented by the bodhisattva Mahamati. In responding to Mahamati's questions, the Buddha expounded many of the essential teachings of Mahayana Buddhism, such as the inner enlightenment that transcends duality and the realization of the *tathagata-garba* (womb of suchness) that is present in all beings.

The basic teachings presented in the *Lankavatara Sutra* were instrumental in shaping Chinese Zen, but they continue to be highly relevant to modern day Zen practice in the West. These teachings explore the nature of mind, self–realization and the process for its attainment, as well as the essential character and stages of development of the bodhisattva. Central to these teachings is the view that words and ideas are not essential for the transmission of the dharma. This view is a reflection of the well-known four tenets that Bodhidharma used to describe Zen. He said "Zen is":

1) A special transmission outside the scriptures
2) With no reliance on words and letters

3) A direct pointing to the human mind
4) And the realization of buddhahood

Bodhidharma was essentially saying that words, letters, and scriptures are at best a description of reality and not the reality itself. The truth of the teachings must be personally realized by each individual, and the only thing sutras — and in fact, Zen teachers — can do, is to directly point to the human mind. This direct pointing is the basis of the ancestral lineage characteristic of Zen. The teachings are transmitted mind to mind from generation to generation from master to disciple.

The nine chapters of prose and verse that comprise the *Lankavatara Sutra* are, in the words of its first English translator, D.T. Suzuki, "A Mahayana text difficult in more than one way to understand perfectly as to its meaning..."

The present epitomized version by Dwight Goddard makes this important sutra more accessible to modern practitioners of Mahayana Buddhism and Zen. Goddard has rendered the text in a form that allows for easier reading, by condensing some sections and omitting parts that are repetitious or too obscure for the modern reader. Goddard skillfully accomplished this abridgment without compromising the full meaning of the text.

Dr. Suzuki's *Studies in the Lankatavara Sutra* was published in 1929 and his translation of the sutra was published in 1932. The essential teachings found in this important primary source have not been readily available in English for many years. The sutra's reappearance in Goddard's epitomized version will return it to its proper place as one of the central sutras in the training of Mahayana Buddhist practitioners.

John Daido Loori
Zen Mountain Monastery
Mt. Tremper, NY
Summer, 2003

Foreword to the 1932 Edition

MATSU, who died in 788, was one of the greatest Zen Masters of the Tang dynasty in China. One evening when he was enjoying the full moon with his disciples, he said: "What do you say, 0 Monks, of this delightful moonlight night?"

Ts'ang said: "Fine night for performing a religious rite."

Hai said: "Fine for all night meditation."

Yuan, without saying a word, quickly left the room. Thereupon the Master remarked: "The Sutra passes to Ts'ang; Zen goes to Hai; as to Yuan, nothing can put him into bondage."

Fa-yen, who died in 1104, was another great Zen Master. He was enjoying an evening with three of his favorite disciples and being engrossed in conversation they forgot how late it was. When they were about to leave, there was no more light to see the way out. The Master, standing in the dark, said: "Each of you make a statement at this junction."

Fo-chien said: "A phoenix is dancing, spreading its multicolored wings against the golden clouds."

Fo-yen said: "An iron colored snake is lying in the ancient pathway."

Fo-kuo said: "Look out for your own footsteps."

The Master concluded: "It is Fo-kuo who will ruin our religion."

Now let me ask, has Mr. Goddard ruined the Sutras? If he had really grasped the meaning (artha), he would not have written it, for no chain of words (ruta) could then have bound him. However, he was too tender hearted, hence this epitomised version. But my warning is: Remember, words are no more than a finger pointing to the moon. Where is the moon now? Watch your step.

Daisetz Teitaro Suzuki

xi

Preface by Dwight Goddard

Professor Suzuki's *Studies In The Lankavatara Sutra* was published in 1929, and his translation of the Lankavatara in 1932 (George Routledge & Son, London). The books awakened a great deal of interest in the Lankavatara which, until these books appeared, had been almost unknown to the European world. They also awakened a great deal of admiration for Professor Suzuki's scholarship and patience in carrying to a conclusion so great a task and in so scholarly a manner.

Owing to the nature of the original Sanskrit text, the English translation is very difficult reading and Professor Suzuki felt, if the Sutra was ever to be read by many general readers, that an editing of it in the interest of easier reading was almost a necessity. For that reason he encouraged the editor to undertake the task, but, of course, Professor Suzuki is in no sense to be held responsible for its character or interpretations.

Under the general rule adopted by the editor, the long introductory chapter, the "meat-eating" chapter, and the chapter on Dharani, were omitted entirely as being later accretions and in no direct sense relating to the theme of the Sutra. The long chapter of verses is also omitted as being obscure and repetitious; and as the essence of the verses is given in the prose sections, they can be omitted without loss for the sake of easier reading. In addition, certain small sections are omitted because of their obscurity, or because they do not appear to add anything to the elucidation of the main thesis.

Under the second rule, the Sutra was cut up into more or less small sections and rearranged into something like an orderly sequence. Under the third rule, these small sections were interwoven and condensed by omitting repetitions, matter that was obscure or tiresomely argumentative. Under the fourth rule, a minimum amount of interpretation was introduced. This was absolutely necessary if the Sutra was to be easily or agreeably read, but the interpretations were confined to matter found within the text itself. Often the author of the Sutra would refer to an important doctrine by a single compound word which if translated would be meaningless to modern occidental ears; in such cases there was nothing else to be done, if the reading was to be easily understood, but to interpret it at more or less length, but I have been scrupulously careful not to do any more than was necessary to bring out the full meaning of the text.

As readers become interested in the Sutra by the reading of this Version they are urged to continue their study of it from the original Sanskrit, or from Prof. Suzuki's books.

Introduction

As an extended introduction to the study of Lankavatara Sutra has been given by Prof. Suzuki in both his studies and translation, only a very brief statement is necessary here.

Nothing is known as to its author, the time of its composition, or as to its original form. There is a myth that it originally consisted of 100,000 verses, and the second chapter of the present text has a footnote which reads: "Here ends the second chapter of the Collection of all the Dharmas, taken from the Lankavatara of 36,000 verses." Apparently it was originally a collection of verses covering all the main teachings of Mahayana Buddhism. This vast collection of verses became a source from which the Masters selected texts for their discourses. As the verses were very epigrammatic, obscure and disconnected, in the course of time the discourses were remembered and the verses largely forgotten, until in the present text there are remaining only 884 verses. The present text has every appearance of being something in the way of a disciple's notebook in which he had written down extracts or outlines of his master's discourses on some of these verses.

It is generally felt that the present text must have been compiled early in the First Century, probably a little earlier than the *Awakening Of Faith* by Ashvagosha, which doctrinally it greatly resembles. The earliest date connected with it is the date of the first Chinese translation made by Dharmaraksha about A.D. 420 and which was lost before 700. Three other Chinese translations have been made: one by Gunabhadra in 443; one by Bodhiruci in 513; and one by Shikshananda about 700. There is also one Tibetan version.

The Sutra has always been a favorite with the Ch'an Sect (Zen, in Japan) and has had a great deal to do with that sect's origin and development. There is a tradition that when Bodhidharma handed over his begging-bowl and robe to his successor that he also gave him his copy of the *Lankavatara*, saying, that he needed no other sutra. In the early days of the Ch'an Sect the Sutra was very much studied, but because of its difficulties and obscurities it gradually dropped out of common use and has been very much neglected for the past thousand years. But during that time many of the great Masters have made it a subject of study and many commentaries have been written upon it. Although other sutras have been more commonly read none have been more influential in fixing the general doctrines of Mahayana Buddhism, and in bringing about the general adoption of Buddhism in China, Korea and Japan.

In closing just a paragraph must be given about the characteristic teachings of the Lankavatara. It is not written as a philosophical treatise is written, to establish a certain system of thought, but was written to elucidate the profoundest experience that comes to the human spirit. It everywhere deprecates dependence upon words and doctrines and urges upon all the wisdom of making a determined effort to attain this highest experience. Again and again it repeats with variations the refrain: "Mahamati, you and all the Bodhisattva-Mahasattvas should avoid the erroneous reasonings of the philosophers and seek this self-realisation of Noble Wisdom." For this reason the Lankavatara is to be classed with the intuitional scriptures of the Orient, rather than with the philosophical literature of the Occident. In China it combined easily with the accepted belief of the Chinese in Laotsu's conception of the Tao and its ethical idealism to make the Buddhism of China and Japan eminently austere and practical, rather than philosophical and emotional.

In the Sutras there are certain Sanskrit words that are of great importance to the understanding of the teaching that are difficult to translate in single words. It seems advisable to speak about them at this time.

Dwight Goddard

Thetford, Vermont, U. S. A.

1932

Glossary

In the interest of the reader unacquainted with Buddhist terminology, Dwight Goddard's original list of Sanskrit terms has been expanded to obviate footnotes in the text.

AKANISHTHA: Lit. "not the least," the particular heavenly domain at the apex of the world of forms *(rupa-loka).*

ALAYA-VIJNANA: Universal or Divine Mind, or all-conserving Mind, used synonymously with Tatha-gata-gargha and Noble Wisdom.

ARHAT: A saint who has realized the goal of Hinayana Buddhism and who, unlike the Bodhisattva, does not defer his own ultimate Realization until all other beings have been Liberated.

ARYA-JNANA: "Noble Knowledge," that which transcends knowledge; Transcendental Intelligence. The word is used synonymously with ARYA-PRAJNA, but signifies the realization-aspect of Noble Wisdom.

ARYA-PRAJNA: "Noble Wisdom." The term is synonymous with all other designations of the ultimate Reality.

BHIKSHU: Monk.

BODHI: The wisdom content of PRAJNA.

BUDDHA: The Perfectly Enlightened One; the One who has fully attained the goal of spiritual unification.

CITTA: Mnd in general.

CITTA-GOCARA: Lit. "mind's cow-pasture," the realm of mind.

DHARMA: Law or Truth; specifically DHARMA has come to be used for the Buddha's Teaching as a whole, and also as Truth in its universal aspect. The term also means "constituent" or "aspect" and in this sense refers to the five doctrinal units: appearances, names, discrimination, right knowledge, and Suchness.

DHARMAKAYA: Truth-body, Truth-principle, Truth-essence. The term is used synonymously with Buddhahood, Tathagatahood, Nirvana, Noble Wisdom, Universal or Divine Mind, to refer to the Ultimate Reality as being universal, undifferentiated, harmonious, and inscrutable.

DHYANA: Meditation or contemplation, generally used synonymously with SAMADHI

DRISHTI: Lit. "sight," the visible realm of manifest existence.

JNANA: The knowledge, cognition, or thinking content of PRAJNA.

KARMA: Lit. "action," the process and law of moral retribution.
KARUNA: The love or compassion content of PRAJNA.

KOTI: Ten million.

MAHASATTVA: Lit. "great being," a synonym of BODHISATTVA.

MANAS: The intuitive mind; the connecting link between the Universal Mind and the individual, conscious, or discriminating mind.

MANO-VIJNANA: The conscious, perceiving, discriminating, thinking intellect.

MAYA: Illusion; the universe of duality.

NAIRATMYA: Egolessness; the absence of an abiding self or essence in subjects and objects.

NIRVANA: The Ultimate Reality.

PARAMITA: An ideal of spiritual perfection, guiding the Way of the *Bodhisattva.* Generally six such ideals are distinguished: open-handedness, discipline, patience, will-power, meditation, and wisdom; these have to be practiced to perfection.

PARINIRVANA: The ultimate form of Realization, perfect cessation of the individual being, coinciding with the death of the body-mind.

PRAJNA: The active aspect of the DHARMAKAYA, the ultimate Principle of unified Love and Wisdom. The word is commonly translated as Wisdom but denotes far more than that, as it includes both the differentiating principle of intellection and the integrating principle of Love; in significance it resembles the Chinese TAO.

SAMADHI: The state of utmost single-mindedness, yielding superlative bliss, of which different degrees are distinguished.

SAMAPATTI: A synonym of SAMADHI, emphasizing the aspect of unification, or merging between subject and object.

SAMSARA: Phenomenal existence, the world of change.

SVABHAVA: The "self-nature" or essence, of which three types are distinguished: wrong discrimination or judgment, relative knowledge, and perfect knowledge.

TUSHITA: The heavenly domain of Bodhisattva Maitreya, the Buddha-to-be.

VAJRAVIMBOPAMA: The highest form of SAMADHI by which the causes of affliction *(klesha)* are destroyed by the practitioner "as if he wielded a thunderbolt *(vajra)*.

Chapter I

DISCRIMINATION

THUS HAVE I HEARD. The Blessed One once appeared in the Castle of Lanka which is on the summit of Mt. Malaya in the midst of the great Ocean. A great many Bodhisattva-Mahasattvas had miraculously assembled from all the Buddha-lands, and a large number of bhikshus were gathered there. The Bodhisattva-Mahasattvas with Mahamati at their head were all perfect masters of the various Samadhis, the tenfold Self-mastery, the ten Powers, and the six Psychic Faculties. Having been anointed by the Buddha's own hands, they all well understood the significance of the objective world; they all knew how to apply the various means, teachings and disciplinary measures according to the various mentalities and behaviors of beings; they were all thoroughly versed in the five Dharmas, the three Svabhavas, the eight Vijnanas, and the twofold Egolessness.

The Blessed One, knowing of the mental agitations going on in the minds of those assembled (like the surface of the ocean stirred into waves by the passing winds), and his great heart moved by compassion, smiled and said: In the days of old the Tathagatas of the past who were Arhats and fully-enlightened Ones came to the Castle of Lanka on Mount Malaya and discoursed on the Truth of Noble Wisdom that is beyond the reasoning knowledge of the philosophers as well as being beyond the understanding of ordinary disciples and masters; and which is realisable only within the inmost consciousness; for your sakes, I too, would discourse on the same Truth. All that is seen in the world is devoid of effort and action because all things in the world are like a dream, or like an image miraculously projected. This is not comprehended by the philosophers and the ignorant, but those who thus see things see them truthfully. Those who see things otherwise walk in discrimination and, as they depend upon discrimination, they cling to dualism. The world as seen by discrimination is like seeing one's own image reflected in a mirror, or one's shadow, or the moon reflected in water, or an echo heard in the valley. People grasping their own shadows of discrimination become attached to this thing and that thing and failing to abandon dualism they go on forever discriminating and thus never attain tranquility. By tranquility is meant Oneness, and Oneness gives birth to the highest Samadhi which is gained by entering into the realm of Noble Wisdom that is realisable only within one's inmost consciousness.

Then all the Bodhisattva-Mahasattvas rose from their seats and respectfully paid him homage and Mahamati the Bodhisattva-Mahasattva sustained by the power of the Buddhas drew his upper garment over one shoulder, knelt and pressing his hands together, praised him in the following verses:

As thou reviewest the world with thy perfect intelligence and compassion, it must seem to thee like an ethereal flower of which one cannot say: it is born, it is destroyed, for the terms being and non-being do not apply to it.

As thou reviewest the world with thy perfect intelligence and compassion, it must seem to thee like a dream of which it cannot be said: it is permanent or it is destructible, for being and non-being do not apply to it.

As thou reviewest all things by thy perfect intelligence and compassion, they must seem to thee like visions beyond the reach of the human mind, as being and non-being do not apply to them.

With thy perfect intelligence and compassion which are beyond all limit, thou comprehendest the Egolessness of things and persons, and art free and clear from the hindrances of passion and learning and egoism.

Thou dost not vanish into Nirvana, nor does Nirvana abide in thee, for Nirvana transcends all duality of knowing and known, of being and non-being.

Those who see thee thus, serene and beyond conception, will be emancipated from attachment, will be cleansed of all defilement, both in this world and in the spiritual world beyond.

in this world whose nature is like a dream, there is place for praise and blame, but in the ultimate Reality of Dharmakaya which is far beyond the senses and the discriminating mind, what is there to praise? 0 thou most Wise!

THEN SAID MAHAMATI the Bodhisattva-Mahasattva: 0 blessed One, Sugata, Arhat and Fully-enlightened One, pray tell us about the realisation of Noble Wisdom which is beyond the path and usage of the philosophers; which is devoid of all predicates such as being and non-being, oneness and otherness, bothness and not-bothness, existence and non-existence, eternity and non-eternity; which has nothing to do with individuality and generality, nor false-imagination, nor any illusions arising from the mind itself; but which manifests itself as the Truth of Highest Reality. By which, going up continuously by the stages of purification, one enters at last upon the stage of Tathagatahood, whereby, by the power of his original vows unattended by any striving, one will radiate its influence to infinite worlds, like a gem reflecting its variegated colors, whereby I and other Bodhisattva-Mahasattvas will be enabled to bring all beings to the same perfection of virtue.

Said the Blessed One: Well done, well done, Mahamati! And again, well done, indeed! It is because of your compassion for the world, because of the benefit it will bring to many people both human kind and celestial, that you have presented yourself before us to make this request. Therefore, Mahamati, listen well and truly reflect upon what I shall say, for I will instruct you.

Then Mahamati and the other Bodhisattva-Mahasattvas gave devout attention to the teaching of the Blessed One.

Mahamati, since the ignorant and simple-minded, not knowing that the world is only something seen of the mind itself, cling to the multitudinousness of external objects, cling to the notions of being and non-being, oneness and otherness, bothness and not-both-ness,

4

existence and non-existence, eternity and noneternity, and think that they have a self-nature of their own, all of which rises from the discriminations of the mind and is perpetuated by habit-energy, and from which they are given over to false imagination. It is all like a mirage in which springs of water are seen as if they were real. They are thus imagined by animals who, made thirsty by the heat of the season, run after them. Animals, not knowing that the springs are an hallucination of their own minds, do not realise that there are no such springs. In the same way, Mahamati, the ignorant and simple-minded, their minds burning with the fires of greed, anger and folly, finding delight in a world of multitudinous forms, their thoughts obsessed with ideas of birth, growth and destruction, not well understanding what is meant by existent and non-existent, and being impressed by the erroneous discriminations and speculations since beginningless time, fall into the habit of grasping this and that and thereby becoming attached to them.

It is like the city of the Gandharvas which the unwitting take to be a real city though it is not so in fact. The city appears as in a vision owing to their attachment to the memory of a city preserved in the mind as a seed; the city can thus be said to be both existent and non-existent. In the same way, clinging to the memory of erroneous speculations and doctrines accumulated since beginningless time, they hold fast to such ideas as oneness and otherness, being and non-being, and their thoughts are not at all clear as to what after all is only seen of the mind. It

5

is like a man dreaming in his sleep of a country that seems to be filled with various men, women, elephants, horses, cars, pedestrians, villages, towns, hamlets, cows, buffalos, mansions, woods, mountains, rivers and lakes, and who moves about in that city until he is awakened. As he lies half awake, he recalls the city of his dreams and reviews his experiences there; what do you think, Mahamati, is this dreamer who is letting his mind dwell upon the various unrealities he has seen in his dream, — is he to be considered wise or foolish? In the same way, the ignorant and simple-minded who are favorably influenced by the erroneous views of the philosophers do not recognise that the views that are influencing them are only dream-like ideas originating in the mind itself, and consequently they are held fast by their notions of oneness and otherness, of being and non-being. It is like a painter's canvas on which the ignorant imagine they see the elevations and depressions of mountains and valleys.

In the same way there are people today being brought up under the influence of similar erroneous views of oneness and otherness, of bothness and notbothness, whose mentality is being conditioned by the habit-energy of these false-imaginings and who later on will declare those who hold the true doctrine of no-birth which is free from the alternatives of being and non-being, to be nihilists and by so doing will bring themselves and others to ruin. By the natural law of cause and effect these followers of pernicious views uproot meritorious causes that otherwise would lead to unstained purity. They are to be shunned by those whose desires are for more excellent things.

It is like the dim-eyed ones who seeing a hairnet exclaim to one another: "It is wonderful! Look, Honorable Sirs, it is wonderful!" But the hairnet has never existed; in fact, it is neither an entity, nor a nonentity, for it has both been seen and has not been seen. In the same manner those whose minds have been addicted to the discriminations of the erroneous views cherished by the philosophers which are given over to the realistic views of being and non-being, will contradict the good Dharma and will end in the destruction of themselves and others.

It is like a wheel of fire made by a revolving fire-brand which is no wheel but which is imagined to be one by the ignorant. Nor is it not-a-wheel because it has not been seen by some. By the same reasoning, those who are in the habit of listening to the discriminations and views of the philosophers will regard things born as non-existent and those destroyed by causation as existent. It is like a mirror reflecting colors and images as determined by conditions but without any partiality. It is like the echo of the wind that gives the sound of a human voice. It is like a mirage of moving water seen in a desert. In the same way the discriminating mind of the ignorant which has been heated by false-imaginations and speculations is stirred into mirage-like waves by the winds of birth, growth and destruction. It is like the magician Pisaca, who by means of his spells makes a wooden image or a dead body to throb with life, though it has no power of its own. In the same way the ignorant and the simpleminded, committing themselves to erroneous philosophical views become thoroughly devoted to the ideas of oneness and otherness, but their confidence is not well grounded. For this reason, Mahamati, you and other Bodhisattva-Mahasattvas should cast off all discriminations leading to the notions of birth, abiding and destructions, of oneness and otherness, of bothness and not-bothness, of being and non-being and thus getting free of the bondage of habit-energy become able to attain the reality realisable within yourselves of Noble Wisdom.

*

THEN SAID MAHAMATI to the Blessed One: Why is it that the ignorant are given up to discrimination and the wise are not?

The Blessed One replied: It is because the ignorant cling to names, signs and ideas; as their minds move along these channels they feed on multiplicities of objects and fall into the notion of an ego-soul and what belongs to it; they make discriminations of good and bad among appearances and cling to the agreeable. As they thus cling there is a reversion to ignorance, and karma born of greed, anger and folly, is accumulated. As the accumulation of karma goes on they become imprisoned in a cocoon of discrimination and are thenceforth unable to free themselves from the round of birth and death.

Because of folly they do not understand that all things are like maya, like the reflection of the moon in water, that there is no self-substance to be imagined as an ego-soul and its belongings, and that all their definitive ideas rise from their false discriminations of what exists only as it is seen of the mind itself. They do not realise that things have nothing to do with qualified and qualifying, nor with the course of birth, abiding and destruction, and instead they assert that they are born of a creator, of time, of atoms, of some celestial spirit. It is because the ignorant are given up to discrimination that they move along with the stream of appearances, but it is not so with the wise.

Chapter II

FALSE-IMAGINATION AND

KNOWLEDGE OF APPEARANCES

THEN MAHAMATI the Bodhisattva-Mahasattva spoke to the Blessed One, saying: You speak of the erroneous views of the philosophers, will you please tell us of them, that we may be on our guard against them?

The Blessed One replied, saying: Mahamati, the error in these erroneous teachings that are generally held by the philosophers lies in this: they do not recognise that the objective world rises from the mind itself; they do not understand that the whole mind-system also rises from the mind itself; but depending upon these manifestations of the mind as being real they go on discriminating them, like the simple-minded ones that they are, cherishing the dualism of this and that, of being and non-being, ignorant of the fact that there is but one common Essence.

On the contrary my teaching is based upon the recognition that the objective world, like a vision, is a manifestation of the mind itself; it teaches the cessation of ignorance, desire, deed and causality; it teaches the cessation of suffering that arises from the discriminations of the triple world.

There are some Brahman scholars who, assuming something out of nothing, assert that there is a substance bound up with causation which abides in time, and that the elements that make up personality and its environment have their genesis and continuation in causation and after thus existing, pass away. Then there are other scholars who hold a destructive and nihilistic view concerning such subjects as continuation, activity, breaking-up, existence, Nirvana, the Path, karma, fruition and Truth. Why? Because they have not attained an intuitive understanding of Truth itself and therefore they have no clear insight into the fundamentals of things. They are like a jar broken into pieces which is no longer able to function as a jar; they are like a burnt seed which is no longer capable of sprouting. But the elements that make up personality and its environment which they regard as subject to change are really incapable of uninterrupted transformations. Their views are based upon erroneous discriminations of the objective world; they are not based upon the true conception.

Again, if it is true that something comes out of nothing and there is the rise of the mind-system by reason of the combination of the three effect-producing causes, we could say the same of any non-existing thing: for instance, that a tortoise could grow hair, or sand produce oil. This proposition is of no avail; it ends in affirming nothing. It follows that the deed, work and cause of which they speak is of no use, and so also is their reference to being and non-being. If they argue that there is a combination of the three effect-producing causes, they must do it on the principle of cause and effect, that is, that something comes out of something and not out of nothing. As long as a world of relativity is asserted, there is an ever recurring chain of causation which cannot be denied under any circumstance, therefore we cannot talk of anything coming to an end or of cessation. As long as these scholars remain on their philosophical ground their demonstration must conform to logic and their textbooks, and the memory-habit of erroneous intellection will ever cling to them. To make the matter worse, the simple-minded ones, poisoned by this erroneous view, will declare this incorrect way of thinking taught by the ignorant, to be the same as that presented by the All-knowing One.

But the way of instruction presented by the Tathagatas is not based on assertions and refutations by means of words and logic. There are four forms of assertion that can be made concerning things not in existence, namely, assertions made about individual marks that are not in existence; about objects that are not in existence; about a cause that is non-existent; and about philosophical views that are erroneous. By refutation is meant that one, because of ignorance, has not examined properly the error that lies at the base of these assertions.

The assertion about individual marks that really have no existence, concerns the distinctive marks as perceived by the eye, ear, nose, etc., as indicating individuality and generality in the elements that make up personality and its external world; and then, taking these marks for reality and getting attached to them, to get into the habit of affirming that things are just so and not otherwise.

The assertion about objects that are non-existent is an assertion that rises from attachment to these associated marks of individuality and generality. Objects in themselves are neither in existence nor in non-existence and are quite devoid of the alternative of being and non-being, and should only be thought of as one thinks of the horns of a hare, a horse, or a camel, which never existed. Objects are discriminated by the ignorant who are addicted to assertion and negation, because their intelligence has not been acute enough to penetrate into the truth that there is nothing but what is seen of the mind itself.

The assertion of a cause that is non-existent assumes the causeless birth of the first element of the mind-system which later on comes to have only a maya-like non-existence. That is to say, there are philosophers who assert that an originally un-born mind-system begins to function under the conditions of eye, form, light and memory, which functioning goes on for a time and then ceases. This is an example of a cause that is non-existent.

The assertion of philosophical views concerning the elements that make up personality and its environing world that are non-existent, assume the existence of an ego, a being, a soul, a living being, a "nourisher," or a spirit. This is an example of philosophical views that are not true.

It is this combination of discrimination of imaginary marks of individuality, grouping them and giving them a name and becoming attached to them as objects, by reason of habit-energy that has been accumulating since beginningless time, that one builds up erroneous views whose only basis is false-imagination. For this reason Bodhisattvas should avoid all discussions relating to assertions and negations whose only basis is words and logic.

Word-discrimination goes on by the coordination of brain, chest, nose, throat, palate, lips, tongue, teeth and lips. Words are neither different nor not-different from discrimination. Words rise from discrimination as their cause; if words were different from discrimination they could not have discrimination for their cause; then again, if words are not different, they could not carry and express meaning. Words, therefore, are produced by causation and are mutually conditioning and shifting and, just like things, are subject to birth and destruction.

There are four kinds of word discrimination, all of which are to be avoided because they are alike unreal. First there are the words indicating individual marks which rise from discriminating forms and signs as being real in themselves and, then, becoming attached to them. There are memory-words which rise from the unreal surroundings which come before the mind when it recalls some previous experience. Then there are words growing out of attachment to the erroneous distinctions and speculations of the mental processes. And finally, there are words growing out of inherited prejudices as seeds of habit-energy have accumulated since beginningless time, or which had their origin in some long forgotten clinging to false-imagination and erroneous speculations.

Then there are words where there are no corresponding objects, as for instance, the hare's horns, a barren woman's child, etc — there are no such things but we have the words, just the same. Words are an artificial creation; there are Buddha-lands where there are no words. In some Buddha-lands ideas are indicated by looking steadily, in others by gestures, in still others by a frown, by a movement of the eyes, by laughing, by yawning, by the clearing of the throat, or by trembling. For instance, in the Buddha-land of the Tathagata Samantabhadra, Bodhisattvas, by a dhyana transcending words and ideas, attain the recognition of all things as un-born and they, also, experience various most excellent Samadhis that transcend words. Even in this world such specialised beings as ants and bees carry on their activities very well without recourse to words. No, Mahamati, the validity of things is independent of the validity of words.

Moreover, there are other things that belong to words, namely, the syllable-body of words, the name-body of words, and the sentence-body of words. By syllable-body is meant that by which words and sentences are set up or indicated: there is a reason for some syllables, some are mnemonic, and some are chosen arbitrarily. By name-body is meant the object depending upon which a name-word obtains its significance, or in other words, name-body is the "substance" of a name-word. By sentence-body is meant the completion of the meaning by expressing the word more fully in a sentence. The name for this sentence-body is suggested by the footprints left in the road by elephants, horses, people, deer, cattle, goats, etc. But neither words nor sentences can exactly express meanings, for words are only sweet sounds that are arbitrarily chosen to represent things, they are not the things themselves, which in turn are only manifestations of mind. Discrimination of meaning is based upon the false-imagination that these sweet sounds which we call words and which are dependent upon whatever subjects they are supposed to stand for, and which subjects are supposed to be self-existent, all of which is based on error. Disciples should be on their guard against the seductions of words and sentences and their illusive meanings, for by them the ignorant and the dull-witted become entangled and helpless as an elephant floundering about in the deep mud.

Words and sentences are produced by the law of causation and are mutually conditioning, — they cannot express highest Reality. Moreover, in highest Reality there are no differentiations to be discriminated and there is nothing to be predicated in regard to it. Highest Reality is an exalted state of bliss, it is not a state of word-discrimination and it cannot be entered into by mere statements concerning it. The Tathagatas have a better way of teaching, namely, through self-realisation of Noble Wisdom.

*

MAHAMATI ASKED the Blessed One: Pray tell us about the causation of all things whereby I and other Bodhisattvas may see into the nature of causation and may no more discriminate it as to the gradual or simultaneous rising of all things?

The Blessed One replied: There are two factors of causation by reason of which all things come into seeming existence: — external and internal factors. The external factors are a lump of clay, a stick, a wheel, a thread, water, a worker, and his labor, the combination of all of which produces a jar. As with a jar which is made from a lump of clay, or a piece of cloth made from thread, or matting made from fragrant grass, or a sprout growing out of a seed, or fresh butter made from sour milk by a man churning it; so it is with all things which appear one after another in continuous succession. As regards the inner factors of causation, they are of such kinds as ignorance, desire, purpose, all of which enter into the idea of causation. Born of these two factors there is the manifestation of personality and the individual things that make up its environment, but they are not individual and distinctive things: they are only so discriminated by the ignorant.

Causation may be divided into six elements: indifference-cause, dependence-cause, possibility-cause, agency-cause, objectivity-cause, manifesting-cause. Indifference-cause means that if there is no discrimination present, there is no power of combination present and so no combination takes place, or if present there is dissolution. Dependence-cause means that the elements must be present. Possibility-cause means that when a cause is to become effective there must be a suitable meeting of conditions both internal and external. Agency-cause means that there must be a principle vested with supreme authority like a sovereign king present and asserting itself. Objectivity-cause means that to be a part of the objective world the mind-system must be in existence and must be keeping up its continuous activity. Manifesting-cause means that as the discriminating faculty of the mind-system becomes busy individual marks will be revealed as forms are revealed by the light of a lamp.

All causes are thus seen to be the outcome of discrimination carried on by the ignorant and simple-minded, and there is, therefore, no such thing as gradual or simultaneous rising of existence. If such a thing as the gradual rising of existence is asserted, it can be disproved by showing that there is no basic substance to hold the individual signs together which makes a gradual rising impossible. If simultaneous rising of existence is asserted, there would be no distinction between cause and effect and there will be nothing to characterise a cause as such. While a child is not yet born, the term father has no significance. Logicians argue that there is that which is born and that which gives birth by the mutual functioning of such causal factors as cause, substance, continuity, acceleration, etc., and so they conclude that there is a gradual rising of existence; but this gradual rising does not obtain except by reason of attachment to the notion of self-nature.

When ideas of body, property and abode are seen, discriminated and cherished in what after all is nothing but what is conceived by the mind itself, an external world is perceived under the aspects of individuality and generality which, however, are not realities, and, therefore, neither a gradual nor a simultaneous rising of things is possible. It is only when the mind-system comes into activity and discriminates the manifestations of mind that existence can be said to come into view. For these reasons, Mahamati, you must get rid of notions of gradation and simultaneity in the combination of causal activities.

*

MAHAMATI SAID: Blessed One, To what kind of discrimination and to what kind of thoughts should the term, false-imagination, be applied?

The Blessed One replied: So long as people do not understand the true nature of the objective world, they fall into the dualistic view of things. They imagine the multiplicity of external objects to be real and become attached to them and are nourished by their habit-energy. Because of this a system of mentation—mind and what belongs to it—is discriminated and is thought of as real; this leads to the assertion of an ego-soul and its belongings, and thus the mind-system goes on functioning. Depending upon and attaching itself to the dualistic habit of mind, they accept the views of the philosophers founded upon these erroneous distinctions, of being and non-being, existence and non-existence, and there evolves what we call, false-imaginations.

But, Mahamati, discrimination does not evolve nor is it put away because, when all that is seen is truly recognised to be nothing but the manifestation of mind, how can discrimination as regards being and non-being evolve? It is for the sake of the ignorant who are addicted to the discrimination of the multiplicity of things which are of their own mind, that it is said by me that discrimination takes its rise owing to attachment to the aspect of multiplicity which is characteristic of objects. How otherwise can the ignorant and simple-minded recognize that there is nothing but what is seen of the mind itself, and how otherwise can they gain an insight into the true nature of mind and be able to free themselves from wrong conceptions of cause and effect? How otherwise can they gain a clear conception of the Bodhisattva stages, and attain a "turning-about" in the deepest seat of their consciousness, and finally attain an inner self-realisation of Noble Wisdom which transcends the five Dharmas, the three Self-natures, and the whole idea of a discriminated Reality? For this reason is it said by me that discrimination takes its rise from the mind becoming attached to the multiplicities of things which in themselves are not real, and that emancipation comes from thoroughly understanding the meaning of Reality as it truly is.

False-imaginations rise from the consideration of appearances: things are discriminated as to form, signs and shape; as to having color, warmth, humidity, motility or rigidity. False-imagination consists in becoming attached to these appearances and their names. By attachment to objects is meant, the getting attached to inner and outer things as if they were real. By attachment to names is meant, the recognition in these inner and outer things of the characteristic marks of individuation and generality, and to regard them as definitely belonging to the names of the objects.

False-imagination teaches that because all things are bound up with causes and conditions of habit energy that has been accumulating since beginningless time by not recognising that the external world is of mind itself, all things are comprehensible under the aspects of individuality and generality. By reason of clinging to these false-imaginations there is multitudinousness of appearances which are imagined to be real but which are only imaginary. To illustrate: when a magician depending on grass, wood, shrubs and creepers, exercises his art, many shapes and beings take form that are only magically created; sometimes they even make figures that have bodies and that move and act like human beings; they are variously and fancifully discriminated but there is no reality in them; everyone but children and the simple-minded know that they are not real. Likewise based upon the notion of relativity false-imagination perceives a variety of appearances which the discriminating mind proceeds to objectify and name and become attached to, and memory and habit-energy perpetuate. Here is all that is necessary to constitute the self-nature of false-imagination.

The various features of false-imagination can be distinguished as follows: as regards words, meaning, individual marks, property, self-nature, cause, philosophical views, reasoning, birth, no-birth, dependence, bondage and emancipation. Discrimination of words is the becoming attached to various sounds carrying familiar meanings. Discrimination of meaning comes when one imagines that words rise depending upon whatever subjects they express, and which subjects are regarded as self-existent. Discrimination of individual marks is to imagine that whatever is denoted in words concerning the multiplicities of individual marks (which in themselves are like a mirage) is true, and clinging tenaciously to them, to discriminate all things according to such categories as, warmth, fluidity, motility, and solidity. Discrimination of property is to desire a state of wealth, such as gold, silver, and various precious stones.

Discrimination of self-nature is to make discriminations according to the views of the philosophers in reference to the self-nature of all things which they imagine and stoutly maintain to be true, saying: "This is just what it is and it cannot be otherwise." Discrimination of cause is to distinguish the notion of causation in reference to being and non-being and to imagine that there are such things as "cause-signs." Discrimination of philosophical views means considering different views relating to the notions of being and non-being, oneness and otherness, bothness and not-both-ness, existence and non-existence, all of which are erroneous, and becoming attached to particular views. Discrimination of reasoning means the teaching whose reasoning is based on the grasping of the notion of an ego-substance and what belongs to it. Discrimination of birth means getting attached to the notion that things come into existence and pass out of existence according to causation. Discrimination of no-birth is to see that causeless substances which were not, come into existence by reason of causation. Discrimination of dependence means the mutual dependence of gold and the filament made of it. Discrimination of bondage and imagination is like imagining that there is something bound because of something binding, as in the case of a man who ties a knot and loosens one.

These are the various features of false-imagination to which all the ignorant and simple-minded cling. Those attached to the notion of relativity are attached to the notion of the multitudinousness of things which arises from false-imagination. It is like seeing varieties of objects depending upon maya, but these varieties thus revealing themselves are discriminated by the ignorant as something other than maya itself, according to their way of thinking. Now the truth is, maya and varieties of objects are neither different nor not different; if they were different, varieties of objects would not have maya for their characteristic; if they are not different there would be no distinction between them. But as there is a distinction these two —

maya and varieties of objects — are neither different nor not-different, for the very good reason: they are one thing.

*

MAHAMATI SAID to the Blessed One: Is error an entity or not? The Blessed One replied: Error has no character in it making for attachment; if error had such a character no liberation would be possible from its attachment to existence, and the chain of origination would only be understood in the sense of creation as upheld by the philosophers. Error is like maya, also, and as maya is incapable from producing other maya, so error in itself cannot produce error; it is discrimination and attachment that produce evil thoughts and faults. Moreover, maya has no power of discrimination in itself; it only rises when invoked by the charm of the magician. Error has in itself no habit-energy; habit-energy only rises from discrimination and attachment. Error in itself has no faults; faults are due to the confused discriminations fondly cherished by the ignorant concerning the ego-soul and its mind. The wise have nothing to do either with maya or error.

Maya, however, is not an unreality because it only has the appearance of reality; all things have the nature of maya. It is not because all things are imagined and clung to because of the multitudinous of individual signs, that they are like maya; it is because they are alike unreal and as quickly appearing and disappearing. Being attached to erroneous thoughts they confuse and contradict themselves and others. As they do not clearly grasp the fact that the world is no more than mind itself, they imagine and cling to causation, work, birth and individual signs, and their thoughts are characterised by error and false-imaginations. The teaching that all things are characterised by the self-nature of maya and a dream is meant to make the ignorant and simple-minded cast aside the idea of self-nature in anything.

False-imagination teaches that such things as light and shade, long and short, black and white are different and are to be discriminated; but they are not independent of each other; they are only different aspects of the same thing, they are terms of relation not of reality. Conditions of existence are not of a mutually exclusive character; in essence things are not two but one. Even Nirvana and Samsara's world of life and death are aspects of the same thing, for there is no Nirvana except where is Samasara, and no Samsara except where is Nirvana. All duality is falsely imagined.

Mahamati, you and all the Bodhisattvas should discipline yourselves in the realisation and patient acceptance of the truths of the emptiness, un-bornness, no self-natureness, and the non-duality of all things. This teaching is found in all the sutras of all the Buddhas and is presented to meet the varied dispositions of all beings, but it is not the Truth itself. These teachings are only a finger pointing toward Noble Wisdom. They are like a mirage with its springs of water which the deer take to be real and chase after. So with the teachings in all the sutras: They are intended for the consideration and guidance of the discriminating minds of all people, but they are not the Truth itself, which can only be self-realised within one's deepest consciousness.

Mahamati, you and all the Bodhisattvas must seek for this inner self-realisation of Noble Wisdom, and be not captivated by word-teaching.

Chapter III

Right Knowledge or Knowledge of Relations

THEN MAHAMATI SAID: Pray tell us, Blessed One, about the being and the non-being of all things?

The Blessed One replied: People of this world are dependent in their thinking on one of two things: on the notion of being whereby they take pleasure in realism, or in the notion of non-being whereby they take pleasure in nihilism; in either case they imagine emancipation where there is no emancipation. Those who are dependent upon the notion of being, regard the world as rising from a causation that is really existent, and that this actually existing and becoming world does not take its rise from a causation that is non-existent. This is the realistic view as held by some people. Then there are other people who are dependent on the notion of the non-being of all things. These people admit the existence of greed, anger and folly, and at the same time they deny the existence of the things that produce greed, anger and folly. This is not rational, for greed, anger and folly are no more to be taken hold of as real than are things; they neither have substance nor individual marks. Where there is a state of bondage, there is binding and means for binding; but where there is emancipation, as in the case of Buddhas, Bodhisattvas, masters and disciples, who have ceased to believe in both being and non-being, there is neither bondage, binding nor means for binding.

It is better to cherish the notion of an ego-substance than to entertain the notion of emptiness derived from the view of being and non-being, for those who so believe fail to understand the fundamental fact that the external world is nothing but a manifestation of mind. Because they see things as transient, as rising from cause and passing away from cause, now dividing, now combining into the elements which make up the aggregates of personality and its external world and now passing away, they are doomed to suffer every moment from the changes that follow one after another, and finally are doomed to ruin.

*

THEN MAHAMATI ASKED the Blessed One, saying: Tell us, Blessed One, how all things can be empty, un-born, and have no self-nature, so that we may be awakened and quickly realise highest enlightenment?

The Blessed One replied: What is emptiness, indeed! It is a term whose very self-nature is false-imagination, but because of one's attachment to false-imagination we are obliged to talk of emptiness, no-birth, and no-self-nature. There are seven kinds of emptiness: emptiness of mutuality which is non-existence; emptiness of individual marks; emptiness of self-nature; emptiness of no-work; emptiness of work; emptiness of all things in the sense that they are unpredicable; and emptiness in its highest sense of Ultimate Reality.

By the emptiness of mutuality which is non-existence is meant that when a thing is missing here, one speaks of its being empty here. For instance: in the lecture hall of Mrigarama there are no elephants present, nor bulls, nor sheep; but as to monks there are many present. We can rightly speak of the hall as being empty as far as animals are concerned. It is not asserted that the lecture hall is empty of its own characteristics, or that the monks are empty of that which makes up their monkhood, nor that in some other place there are no elephants, bulls, nor sheep to be found. In this case we are speaking of things in their aspect of individuality and generality, but from the point of view of mutuality some things do not exist somewhere. This is the lowest form of emptiness and is to be sedulously put away.

By emptiness of individual marks is meant that all things have no distinguishing marks of individuality and generality. Because of mutual relations and interactions things are superficially discriminated but when they are further and more carefully investigated and analysed they are seen to be non-existent and nothing as to individuality and generality can be predicated of them. Thus when individual marks can no longer be seen, ideas of self, otherness and bothness, no longer hold good. So it must be said that all things are empty of self-marks.

By emptiness of self-nature is meant that all things in their self-nature are un-born; therefore, is it said that things are empty as to self-nature. By emptiness of no-work is meant that the aggregate of elements that makes up personality and its external world is Nirvana itself and from the beginning there is no activity in them; therefore, one speaks of the emptiness of no-work. By emptiness of work is meant that the aggregates being devoid of an ego and its belongings, go on functioning automatically as there is mutual conjunction of causes and conditions; thus one speaks of the emptiness of work. By emptiness of all things in the sense that they are unpredicable is meant that, as the very nature of false-imagination is inexpressible, so all things are unpredicable, and, therefore, are empty in that sense. By emptiness in its highest sense of the emptiness of Ultimate Reality is meant that in the attainment of inner self-realisation of Noble Wisdom there is no trace of habit-energy generated by erroneous conceptions; thus one speaks of the highest emptiness of Ultimate Reality.

When things are examined by right knowledge there are no signs obtainable which would characterise them with marks of individuality and generality, therefore, they are said to have no self-nature. Because these signs of individuality and generality are seen both as existing and yet are known to be non-existent, are seen as going out and yet are known not to be going out, they are never annihilated. Why is this true? For this reason; because the individual signs that should make up the self-nature of all things are non-existent. Again in their self-nature things are both eternal and non-eternal. Things are not eternal because the marks of individuality appear and disappear, that is, the marks of self-nature are characterised by non-eternality. On the other hand, because things are un-boi7n and are only mind-made, they are in a deep sense eternal. That is, things are eternal because of their very non-eternality.

Further, besides understanding the emptiness of all things both in regard to substance and self-nature, it is necessary for Bodhisattvas to clearly understand that all things are un-born. It is not asserted that things are not born in a superficial sense, but that in a deep sense they are not born of themselves. All that can be said, is this, that relatively speaking, there is a constant stream of becoming, a momentary and uninterrupted change from one state of appearance to another. When it is recognised that the world as it presents itself is no more than a manifestation of mind, then birth is seen as no-birth and all existing objects, concerning which discrimination asserts that they are and are not, are non-existent and, therefore, un-born; being devoid of agent and action things are un-born.

If things are not born of being and non-being, but are simply manifestations of mind itself, they have no reality, no self-nature: — they are like the horns of a hare, a horse, a donkey, a camel. But the ignorant and the simple-minded, who are given over to their false and erroneous imaginings, discriminate things where they are not. To the ignorant the characteristic marks of the self-nature of body-property-and-abode seem to be fundamental and rooted in the very nature of the mind itself, so they discriminate their multitudinousness and become attached to them.

There are two kinds of attachment: attachment to objects as having self-nature, and attachment to words as having self-nature. The first takes place by not knowing that the external world is only a manifestation of the mind itself; and the second arises from one's clinging to words and names by reason of habit-energy. In the teaching of no-birth, causation is out of place because, seeing that all things are like maya and a dream, one does not discriminate individual signs. That all things are un-born and have no self-nature because they are like maya is asserted to meet the thesis of the philosophers that birth is by causation. They foster the notion that the birth of all things is derived from the concept of being and non-being, and fail to regard it as it truly is, — as caused by attachment to the multitudinousness which arises from discriminations of the mind itself.

Those who believe in the birth of something that has never been in existence and, coming into existence, vanishes away, are obliged to assert that things come to exist and vanish away by causation — such people find no foothold in my teachings. When it is realised that there is nothing born, and nothing passes away, then there is no way to admit being and non-being, and the mind becomes quiescent.

*

THEN MAHAMATI SAID to the Blessed One: The philosophers declare that the world rises from causal agencies according to a law of causation; they state that their cause is unborn and is not to be annihilated. They mention nine primary elements: Ishvara the Creator, the Creation, atoms, etc., which being elementary are unborn and not to be annihilated. The Blessed One, while teaching that all things are un-born and that there is no annihilation, also declares that the world takes its rise from ignorance, discrimination, attachment, deed, etc., working according to a law of causation. Though the two sets of elements may differ in form and name, there does not appear to be any essential difference between the two positions. If there is anything that is distinctive and superior in the Blessed One's teaching, pray tell us, Blessed One, what it is?

The Blessed One replied: My teaching of no-birth and no-annihilation is not like that of the philosophers, nor is it like their doctrine of birth and impermanency. That to which the philosophers ascribe the characteristic of no-birth and no-annihilation is the self-nature of all things, which causes them to fall into the dualism of being and non-being. My teaching transcends the whole conception of being and non-being; it has nothing to do with birth, abiding and destruction; nor with existence and non-existence. I teach that the multitudinousness of objects have no reality in themselves but are only seen of the mind and, therefore, are of the nature of maya and a dream. I teach the non-existence of things because they carry no signs of any inherent self-nature. It is true that in one sense they are seen and discriminated by the senses as individualised objects; but in another sense, because of the absence of any characteristic marks of self-nature, they are not seen but are only imagined. In one sense they are graspable, but in another sense, they are not graspable.

When it is clearly understood that there is nothing in the world but what is seen of the mind itself, discrimination no more rises, and the wise are established in their true abode which is the realm of quietude. The ignorant discriminate and work trying to adjust themselves to external conditions, and are constantly perturbed in mind; unrealities are imagined and discriminated, while realities are unseen and ignored. It is not so with the wise. To illustrate: What the ignorant see is like the magically-created city of the Gandharvas, where children are shown streets and houses, and phantom merchants, and people going in and coming out. This imaginary city with its streets and houses and people going in and coming out, are not thought of as being born or being annihilated, because in their case there is no question as to their existence or non-existence. In like manner, I teach, that there is nothing made nor un-made; that there is nothing that has connection with birth and destruction except as the ignorant cherish falsely imagined notions as to the reality of the external world. When objects are not seen and judged as they truly are in themselves, there is discrimination and clinging to the notions of being and non-being, and individualised self-nature, and as long as these notions of individuality and self-nature persist, the philosophers are bound to explain the external world by a law of causation. This position raises the question of a first cause which the philosophers meet by asserting that their first cause, Ishvara and the primal elements, are un-born and un-annihilate; which position is without evidence and is irrational.

Ignorant people and worldly philosophers cherish a kind of no-birth, but it is not the no-birth which I teach. I teach the un-bornness of the un-born essence of all things which teaching is established in the minds of the wise by their self-realisation of Noble Wisdom. A ladle, clay, a vessel, a wheel, or seeds, or elements— these are external conditions; ignorance discrimination, attachment, habit, karma,—these are inner conditions. When this entire universe is regarded as concatenation and as nothing else but concatenation, then the mind, by its patient acceptance of the truth that all things are un-born, gains tranquillity.

Chapter IV

PERFECT KNOWLEDGE, OR KNOWLEDGE OF REALITY

THEN MAHAMATI ASKED the Blessed One: Pray tell us, Blessed One, about the five Dharmas, so that we may fully understand Perfect Knowledge?

The Blessed One replied: The five Dharmas are: appearance, name, discrimination, right-knowledge and Reality. By appearance is meant that which reveals itself to the senses and to the discriminating-mind and is perceived as form, sound, odour, taste, and touch. Out of these appearances ideas are formed, such as clay, water, jar, etc., by which one says: this is such and such a thing and is no other,—this is name. When appearances are contrasted and names compared, as when we say: this is an elephant, this is a horse, a cart, a pedestrian, a man, a woman, or, this is mind and what belongs to it,—the things thus named are said to be discriminated. As these discriminations come to be seen as mutually conditioning, as empty of self-substance, as un-born, and thus come to be seen as they truly are, that is, as manifestations of the mind itself,—this is right-knowledge. By it the wise cease to regard appearances and names as realities.

When appearances and names are put away and all discrimination ceases, that which remains is the true and essential nature of things and, as nothing can be predicated as to the nature of essence, it is called the "Suchness" of Reality. This universal, undifferentiated, inscrutable, "Suchness" is the only Reality but it is variously characterised as Truth, Mind-essence, Transcendental Intelligence, Noble Wisdom, etc. This Dharma of the imagelessness of the Essence-nature of Ultimate Reality is the Dharma which has been proclaimed by all the Buddhas, and when all things are understood in full agreement with it, one is in possession of Perfect Knowledge, and is on his way to the attainment of the Transcendental Intelligence of the Tathagatas.

*

THEN MAHAMATI SAID to the Blessed One: Are the three self-natures, of things, ideas, and Reality, to be considered as included in the Five Dharmas, or as having their own characteristics complete in themselves.

The Blessed One replied: The three self-natures, the eightfold mind-system, and the twofold egolessness are all included in the Five Dharmas. The self-natures of things, of ideas, and of the sixfold mind-system, correspond with the Dharmas of appearance, name and discrimination; the self-nature of Universal Mind and Reality corresponds to the Dharmas of right-knowledge and "Suchness."

By becoming attached to what is seen of the mind itself, there is an activity awakened which is perpetuated by habit-energy that becomes manifest in the mind-system. From the activities of the mind-system there rises the notion of an ego-soul and its belongings; the discriminations, attachments, and notion of an ego-soul, rising simultaneously like the sun and its rays of light.

By the egolessness of things is meant that the elements that make up the aggregates of personality and its objective world being characterised by the nature of maya and destitute of anything that can be called ego-substance, are therefore un-born and have no self-nature. How can *things* be said to have an ego-soul? By the egolessness of persons is meant that in the aggregates that make up personality there is no ego-substance, nor anything that is like ego-substance nor that belongs to it. The mind-system, which is the most characteristic mark of personality, originated in ignorance, discrimination, desire and deed; and its activities are perpetuated by perceiving, grasping and becoming attached to objects as if they were real. The memory of these discriminations, desires, attachments and deeds is stored in Universal Mind since beginning-less time, and is still being accumulated where it conditions the appearance of personality and its environment and brings about constant change and destruction from moment to moment. The manifestations are like a river, a seed, a lamp, a cloud, the wind; Universal mind in its voraciousness to store up everything, is like a monkey never at rest, like a fly ever in search of food and without partiality, like a fire that is never satisfied, like a water-lifting machine that goes on rolling. Universal mind as defiled by habit-energy is like a magician that causes phantom things and people to appear and move about. A thorough understanding of these things is necessary to an understanding of the egolessness of persons.

There are four kinds of Knowledge: Appearance-knowledge, relative knowledge, perfect-knowledge, and Transcendental Intelligence. Appearance-knowledge belongs to the ignorant and simple-minded who are addicted to the notion of being and non-being, and who are frightened at the thought of being unborn. It is produced by the concordance of the triple combination and attaches itself to the multiplicities of objects; it is characterised by attainability and accumulation; it is subject to birth and destruction. Appearance-knowledge belongs to word-mongers who revel in discriminations, assertions and negations.

Relative-knowledge belongs to the mind-world of the philosophers. It rises from the mind's ability to consider the relations which appearances bear to each other and to the mind considering them, it rises from the mind's ability to arrange, combine and analyse these relations by its powers of discursive logic and imagination, by reason of which it is able to peer into the meaning and significance of things.

Perfect-knowledge belongs to the world of the Bodhisattvas who recognise that all things are but manifestations of mind; who clearly understand the emptiness, the un-bornness, the egolessness of all things; and who have entered into an understanding of the Five Dharmas, the twofold egolessness, and into the truth of imagelessness. Perfect-knowledge differentiates the Bodhissattva stages, and is the pathway and the entrance into the exalted state of self-realisation of Noble Wisdom.

Perfect-knowledge (*jnana*) belongs to the Bodhisattvas who are entirely free from the dualisms of being and non-being, no-birth and no-annihilation, all assertions and negations, and who, by reason of self-realisation, have gained an insight into the truths of egolessness and imagelessness. They no longer discriminate the world as subject to causation: they regard the causation that rules the world as something like the fabled city of the Gandharvas. To them the world is like a vision and a dream, it is like the birth and death of a barren-woman's child; to them there is nothing evolving and nothing disappearing.

The wise who cherish Perfect-knowledge, may be divided into three classes: disciples, masters and Arhats. Common disciples are separated from masters as common disciples continue to cherish the notion of individuality and generality; masters rise from common disciples when, forsaking the error of individuality and generality, they still cling to the notion of an ego-soul by reason of which they go off by themselves into retirement and solitude. Arhats rise when the error of all discrimination is realised. Error being discriminated by the wise turns into Truth by virtue of the "turning-about" that takes place within the deepest consciousness. Mind, thus emancipated, enters into perfect self-realisation of Noble Wisdom.

But, Mahamati, if you *assert* that there is such a thing as Noble Wisdom, it no longer holds good, because anything of which something is asserted thereby partakes of the nature of being and is thus characterised with the quality of birth. The very assertion: "All things are un-born" destroys the truthfulness of it. The same is true of the statements: "All things are empty, and "All things have no self-nature," — both are untenable when put in the form of assertions. But when it is pointed out that all things are like a dream and a vision, it means that in one way things are perceived, and in another way they are not perceived; that is, in ignorance they are perceived but in Perfect-knowledge they are not perceived. All assertions and negations being thought constructions are un-born. Even the assertion that Universal Mind and Noble Wisdom are Ultimate Reality, is thought construction and, therefore, is un-born. As "things" there is no Universal Mind, there is no Noble Wisdom, there is no Ultimate Reality. The insight of the wise who move about in the realm of imagelessness and its solitude is pure. That is, for the wise all "things" are wiped away and even the state of imagelessness ceases to exist.

Chapter V

THE MIND SYSTEM

THEN MAHAMATI SAID to the Blessed One: Pray tell us, Blessed One, what is meant by the mind *(citta)?*

The Blessed One replied: All things of this world, be they seemingly good or bad, faulty or faultless, effect-producing or not effect-producing, receptive or non-receptive, may be divided into two classes: evil out-flowings and the non out-flowing good. The five grasping elements that make up the aggregates of personality, namely, form, sensation, perception, discrimination, and consciousness, and that are imagined to be good and bad, have their rise in the habit-energy of the mind-system, — they are the evil out-flowings of life. The spiritual attainments and the joys of the Samadhis and the fruitage of the Samapattis that come to the wise through their self-realisation of Noble Wisdom and that culminate in their return and participation in the relations of the triple world are called the non out-flowing good.

The mind-system which is the source of the evil out-flowings consists of the five sense-organs and their accompanying sense-minds *(vijnanas)* all of which are unified in the discriminating-mind *(manovijnana).* There is an unending succession of sense-concepts flowing into this discriminating or thinking-mind which combines them and discriminates them and passes judgement upon them as to their goodness or badness. Then follows aversion to or desire for them and attachment and deed; thus the entire system moves on continuously and closely bound together. But it fails to see and understand that what it sees and discriminates and grasps is only a manifestation of its own activity and has no other basis, and so the mind goes on erroneously perceiving and discriminating differences of forms and qualities, not remaining still even for a minute.

In the mind-system there are three modes of activity distinguishable: the sense-minds functioning while remaining in their original nature, the sense-minds as producing effects, and the sense-minds as evolving. By normal functioning the sense-minds grasp appropriate elements of their external world, by which sensation and perception arise at once and by degrees in every sense-organ and every sense-mind, in the pores of the skin, and even in the atoms that make up the body, by which the whole field is apprehended like a mirror reflecting objects, and not realising that the external world itself is only a manifestation of mind. The second mode of activity produces effects by which these sensations react on the discriminating mind to produce perceptions, attractions, aversions, grasping, deed and habit. The third mode of activity has to do with the growth, development and passing of the mind-system, that is, the mind-system is in subjection to its own habit-energy accumulated from beginningless time, as for instance: the "eyeness in the eye that predisposes it to grasp and become attached to multiple forms and appearances. In this way the activities of the evolving mind-system by reason of its habit-energy stirs up waves of objectivity on the face of Universal Mind which in turn conditions the activities and evolvement of the mind-system. Appearances, perception, attraction, grasping, deed, habit, reaction, condition one another incessantly, and the functioning sense-minds, the discriminating-mind and Universal Mind are thus bound up together. Thus, by reason of discrimination of that which by nature is maya-like and unreal false-imagination and erroneous reasoning takes place, action follows and its habit-energy accumulates thereby defiling the pure face of Universal Mind, and as a result the mind-system comes into functioning and the physical body has its genesis. But the discriminating-mind has no thought that by its discriminations and attachments it is conditioning the whole body and so the sense-minds and the discriminating-mind go on mutually related and mutually conditioned in a most intimate manner and building up a world of representations out of the activities of its own imagination. As a mirror reflects forms, the perceiving senses perceive appearances which the discriminating-mind gathers together and proceeds to discriminate, to name and become attached to. Between these two functions there is no gap, nevertheless, they are mutually conditioning. The perceiving senses grasp that for which they have an affinity, and there is a transformation takes place in their structure by reason of which the mind proceeds to combine, discriminate, apprise, and act; then follows habit-energy and the establishing of the mind and its continuance.

The discriminating-mind because of its capacity to discriminate, judge, select and reason about, is also called the thinking, or intellectual-mind. There are three divisions of its mental activity: mentation which functions in connection with attachment to objects and ideas, mentation that functions in connection with general ideas, and mentation that examines into the validity of these general ideas. The mentation which functions in connection with attachment to objects and ideas derived from discrimination, discriminates the mind from its mental processes and accepts the ideas from it as being real and becomes attached to them. A variety of false judgements are thus arrived at as to being, multiplicity, individuality, value, etc., a strong grasping takes place which is perpetuated by habit-energy and thus discrimination goes on asserting itself.

These mental processes give rise to general conceptions of warmth, fluidity, motility, and solidity, as characterising the objects of discrimination, while the tenacious holding to these general ideas gives rise to proposition, reason, definition, and illustration, all of which lead to the assertions of relative knowledge and the establishment of confidence in birth, self-nature, and an ego-soul.

By mentation as an examining function is meant the intellectual act of examining into these general conclusions as to their validity, significance, and truthfulness. This is the faculty that leads to understanding, right-knowledge and points the way to self-realisation.

*

THEN MAHAMATI SAID to the Blessed One: Pray tell us, Blessed One, what relation ego-personality bears to the mind-system?

The Blessed One replied: To explain it, it is first necessary to speak of the self-nature of the five grasping aggregates that make up personality, although as I have already shown they are empty, un-born, and without self-nature. These five grasping aggregates are: form, sensation, perception, discrimination, consciousness. Of these, form

44

belongs to what is made of the so-called primary elements, whatever they may be. The four remaining aggregates are without form and ought not to be reckoned as four, because they merge imperceptibly into one another. They are like space which cannot be numbered; it is only due to imagination that they are discriminated and likened to space. Because things are endowed with appearances of being, characteristic-marks, perceivableness, abode, work, one can say that they are born of effect-producing causes, but this can not be said of these four intangible aggregates for they are without form and marks. These four mental aggregates that make up personality are beyond calculability, they are beyond the four propositions, they are not to be predicated as existing nor as not existing, but together they constitute what is known as mortal-mind. They are even more maya-like and dream-like than are things, nevertheless, as discriminating mortal-mind they obstruct the self-realisation of Noble Wisdom. But it is only by the ignorant that they are enumerated and thought of as an ego-personality; the wise do not do so. This discrimination of the five aggregates that make up personality and that serve as a basis for an ego-soul and ground for its desires and self-interests must be given up, and in its place the truth of imagelessness and solitude should be established.

*

THEN SAID MAHAMATI to the Blessed One: Pray tell us, Blessed One, about Universal Mind and its relation to the lower mind-system?

The Blessed One replied: The sense-minds and their centralised discriminating-mind are related to the external world which is a manifestation of itself and is given over to perceiving, discriminating, and grasping its maya-like appearances. Universal Mind (*Alaya-vijnana*) transcends all individuation and limits. Universal Mind is thoroughly pure in its essential nature, subsisting unchanged and free from faults of impermanence, undisturbed by egoism, unruffled by distinctions, desires and aversions. Universal Mind is like a great ocean, its surface ruffled by waves and surges but its depths remaining forever unmoved. In itself it is devoid of personality and all that belongs to it, but by reason of the defilement upon its face it is like an actor and plays a variety of parts, among which a mutual functioning takes place and the mind-system arises. The principle of intellection becomes divided and mind, the functions of mind, the evil out-flowings of mind, take on individuation. The sevenfold gradation of mind appears: namely, intuitive self-realisation, thinking-desiring-discriminating, seeing, hearing, tasting, smelling, touching, and all their interactions and reactions take their rise.

The discriminating-mind is the cause of the sense-minds and is their support and with them is kept functioning as it describes and becomes attached to a world of objects, and then, by means of its habit-energy, it defiles the face of Universal Mind. Thus Universal Mind becomes the storage and clearing house of all the accumulated products of mentation and action since beginningless time.

Between Universal Mind and the individual discriminating-mind is the intuitive-mind (*manas*) which is dependent upon Universal Mind for its cause and support and enters into relations with both. It partakes of the universality of Universal Mind, shares its purity, and like it, is above form and momentariness. It is through the intuitive-mind that the good non out-flowings emerge, are manifested and are realised. Fortunate it is that intuition is not momentary for if the enlightenment which comes by intuition were momentary the wise would lose their "wiseness" which they do not. But the intuitive-mind enters into relations with the lower mind-system, shares its experiences and reflects upon its activities.

Intuitive-mind is one with Universal Mind by reason of its participation in Transcendental Intelligence *(Arya-jnana)*, and is one with the mind-system by its comprehension of differentiated knowledge *(vijnana)*. Intuitive-mind has no body of its own nor any marks by which it can be differentiated. Universal Mind is its cause and support but it is evolved along with the notion of an ego and what belongs to it, to which it clings and upon which it reflects. Through intuitive-mind, by the faculty of intuition which is a mingling of both identity and perceiving, the inconceivable wisdom of Universal Mind is revealed and made realisable. Like Universal Mind it can not be the source of error.

The discriminating-mind is a dancer and a magician with the objective world as his stage. Intuitive-mind is the wise jester who travels with the magician and reflects upon his emptiness and transiency. Universal Mind keeps the record and knows what must be and what may be. It is because of the activities of the discriminating-mind that error rises and an objective world evolves and the notion of an ego-soul becomes established. If and when the discriminating-mind can be gotten rid of, the whole mind-system will cease to function and Universal Mind will alone remain. Getting rid of the discriminating-mind removes the cause of all error.

*

THEN SAID MAHAMATI to the Blessed One: Pray tell us, Blessed One, what is meant by the cessation of the mind-system?

The Blessed One replied: The five sense-functions and their discriminating and thinking function have their risings and complete endings from moment to moment. They are born with discrimination as cause, with form and appearance and objectivity closely linked together as condition. The will-to-live is the mother, ignorance is the father. By setting up names and forms greed is multiplied and thus the mind goes on mutually conditioning and being conditioned. By becoming attached to names and forms, not realising that they have no more basis than the activities of the mind itself, error rises, false-imagination as to pleasure and pain rises, and the way to emancipation is blocked. The lower system of sense-minds and the discriminating-mind do not really suffer pleasure and pain—they only imagine they do. Pleasure and pain are the deceptive reactions of mortal-mind as it grasps an imaginary objective world.

There are two ways in which the ceasing of the mind-system may take place: as regards form, and as regards continuation. The sense-organs function as regards form by the interaction of form, contact and grasping; and they cease to function when this contact is broken. As regards continuation,—when these interactions of form, contact and grasping cease, there is no more continuation of the seeing, hearing and other sense functions; with the ceasing of these sense functions, the discriminations, graspings and attachments of the discriminating-mind cease; and with their ceasing act and deed and their habit-energy cease, and there is no more accumulation of karma-defilement on the face of Universal Mind.

If the evolving mortal-mind were of the same nature as Universal Mind the cessation of the lower mind-system would mean the cessation of Universal Mind, but they are different for Universal Mind is not the cause of mortal-mind. There is no cessation of Universal Mind in its pure and essence-nature. What ceases to function is not Universal Mind in its essence-nature, but is the cessation of the effect-producing defilements upon its face that have been caused by the accumulation of the habit-energy of the activities of the discriminating and thinking mortal-mind. There is no cessation of Divine Mind which, in itself, is the abode of Reality and the Womb of Truth.

By the cessation of the sense-minds is meant, not the cessation of their perceiving functions, but the cessation of their discriminating and naming activities which are centralised in the discriminating mortal-mind. By the cessation of the mind-system as a whole is meant, the cessation of discrimination, the clearing away of the various attachments, and, therefore, the clearing away of the defilements of habit-energy on the face of Universal Mind which have been accumulating since beginningless time by reason of these discriminations, attachments, erroneous reasonings, and following acts. The cessation of the continuation aspect of the mind-system as a whole, takes place when there is the cessation of that which supports the mind-system, namely, the discriminating mortal-mind. With the cessation of mortal-mind the entire world of maya and desire disappears. Getting rid of the discriminating mortal-mind is Nirvana.

But the cessation of the discriminating-mind can not take place until there has been a "turning-about" in the deepest seat of consciousness. The mental habit of looking outward by the discriminating-mind upon an external objective world must be given up, and a new habit if realising Truth within the intuitive-mind by becoming one with Truth itself must be established. Until this intuitive self-realisation of Noble Wisdom is attained, the evolving mind-system will go on. But when an insight into the five Dharmas, the three self-natures, and the twofold egolessness is attained, then the way will be opened for this "turning-about" to take place. With the ending of pleasure and pain, of conflicting ideas, of the disturbing interests of egoism, a state of tranquillisation will be attained in which the truths of emancipation will be fully understood and there will be no further evil out-flowings of the mind-system to interfere with the perfect self-realisation of Noble Wisdom.

Chapter VI

TRANSCENDENTAL INTELLIGENCE

THEN SAID MAHAMATI: Pray tell us, Blessed One, what constitutes Transcendental Intelligence?

The Blessed One replied: Transcendental Intelligence is the inner state of self-realisation of Noble Wisdom. It is realised suddenly and intuitively as the "turning-about" takes place in the deepest seat of consciousness; it neither enters nor goes out—it is like the moon seen in water. Transcendental Intelligence is not subject to birth nor destruction; it has nothing to do with combination nor concordance; it is devoid of attachment and accumulation; it transcends all dualistic conceptions.

When Transcendental Intelligence is considered, four things must be kept in mind: words, meanings, teachings and Noble Wisdom *(Arya-prajna)*. Words are employed to express meanings but they are dependent upon discriminations and memory as cause, and upon the employment of sounds or letters by which a mutual transference of meaning is possible. Words are only symbols and may or may not clearly and fully express the meaning intended and, moreover, words may be understood quite differently from what was intended by the speaker. Words are neither different nor not different from meaning and meaning stands in the same relation to words.

If meaning is different from words it could not be made manifest by means of words; but meaning is illumined by words as things are by a lamp. Words are just like a man carrying a lamp to look for his property, by which he can say: this is my property. Just so, by means of words and speech originating in discrimination, the Bodhisattva can enter into the meaning of the teachings of the Tathagatas and through the meaning he can enter into the exalted state of self-realisation of Noble Wisdom, which, in itself, is free from word discrimination. But if a man becomes attached to the literal meaning of words and holds fast to the illusion that words and meaning are in agreement, especially in such things as Nirvana which is un-born and un-dying, or as to distinctions of the Vehicles, the five Dharmas, the three self-natures, then he will fail to understand the true meaning and will become entangled in assertions and refutations. Just as varieties of objects are seen and discriminated in dreams and in visions, so ideas and statements are discriminated erroneously and error goes on multiplying.

The ignorant and simple-minded declare that meaning is not otherwise than words, that as words are, so is meaning. They think that as meaning has no body of its own that it cannot be different from words and, therefore, declare meaning to be identical with words. In this they are ignorant of the nature of words, which are subject to birth and death, whereas meaning is not; words are dependent upon letters and meaning is not; meaning is apart from existence and non-existence, it has no substratum, it is unborn. The Tathagatas do not teach a Dharma that is dependent upon letters. Anyone who teaches a doctrine that is dependent upon letters and words is a mere prattler, because Truth is beyond letters and words and books.

This does not mean that words and books never declare what is in conformity with meaning and truth, but it means that words and books are dependent upon discriminations, while meaning and truth are not; moreover, words and books are subject to the interpretation of individual minds, while meaning and truth are not. But if Truth is not expressed in words and books, the scriptures which contain the meaning of Truth would disappear, and when the scriptures disappear there will be no more disciples and masters and Bodhisattvas and Buddhas, and there will be nothing to teach. But no one must become attached to the words of the scriptures because even the canonical texts sometimes deviate from their straightforward course owing to the imperfect functioning of sentient minds. Religious discourses are given by myself and other Tathagatas in response to the varying needs and faiths of all manner of beings, in order to free them from dependence upon the thinking function of the mind-system, but they are not given to take the place of self-realisation of Noble Wisdom. When there is recognition that there is nothing in the world but what is seen of the mind itself, all dualistic discriminations will be discarded and the truth of imagelessness will be understood, and will be seen to be in conformity with meaning rather than with words and letters.

The ignorant and simple-minded being fascinated with their self-imaginations and erroneous reasonings, keep on dancing and leaping about, but are unable to understand the discourse by words about the truth of self-realisation, much less are they able to understand the Truth itself. Clinging to the external world, they cling to the study of books which are a means only, and do not know properly how to ascertain the truth of self-realisation, which is Truth unspoiled by the four propositions. Self-realisation is an exalted state of inner attainment which transcends all dualistic thinking and which is above the mind-system with its logic, reasoning, theorising, and illustrations. The Tathagatas discourse to the ignorant, but sustain the Bodhisattvas as they seek self-realisation of Noble Wisdom.

Therefore, let every disciple take good heed not to become attached to words as being in perfect conformity with meaning, because Truth is not in the letters. When a man with his finger-tip points to something to somebody, the finger-tip may be mistaken for the thing pointed at; in like manner the ignorant and simple-minded, like children, are unable even to the day of their death to abandon the idea that in the finger-tip of words there is the meaning itself. They cannot realise Ultimate Reality because of their intent clinging to words which were intended to be no more than a pointing finger. Words and their discrimination bind one to the dreary round of rebirths into the world of birth-and-death; meaning stands alone and is a guide to Nirvana. Meaning is attained by much learning, and much learning is attained by becoming conversant with meaning and not with words; therefore, let seekers for truth reverently approach those who are wise and avoid the sticklers for particular words.

As for teachings: there are priests and popular preachers who are given to ritual and ceremony and who are skilled in various incantations and in the art of eloquence; they should not be honored nor reverently attended upon, for what one gains from them is emotional excitement and worldly enjoyment; it is not the Dharma. Such preachers, by their clever manipulation of words and phrases and various reasonings and incantations, being the mere prattle of a child, as far as one can make out and not at all in accordance with truth nor in unison with meaning, only serves to awaken sentiment and emotion, while it stupifies the mind. As he himself does not understand the meaning of all things, he only confuses the minds of his hearers with his dualistic views. Not understanding himself, that there is nothing but what is seen of the mind, and himself attached to the notion of self-nature in external things, and unable to know one path from another, he has no deliverance to offer others. Thus these priests and popular preachers who are clever in various incantations and skilled in the art of eloquence, themselves never being emancipated from such calamities as birth, old age, disease, sorrow, lamantation, pain and despair, lead the ignorant into bewilderment by means of their various words, phrases, examples, and conclusions.

Then there are the materialistic philosophers. No respect nor service is to be shown them because their teachings, though they may be explained by using hundreds of thousands of words and phrases, do not go beyond the concerns of this world and this body and in the end they lead to suffering. As the materialists recognise no truth as existing by itself, they are split up into many schools, each of which clings to its own way of reasoning.

But there is that which does not belong to materialism and which is not reached by the knowledge of the philosophers who cling to false-discriminations and erroneous reasonings because they fail to see that, fundamentally, there is no reality in external objects. When it is recognised that there is nothing beyond what is seen of the mind itself, the discrimination of being and non-being ceases and, as there is thus no external world as the object of perception, nothing remains but the solitude of Reality. This does not belong to the materialistic philosophers, it is the domain of the Tathagatas. If such things are imagined as the coming and going of the mind-system, vanishing and appearing, solicitation, attachment, intense affection, a philosophic hypothesis, a theory, an abode, a sense-concept, atomic attraction, organism, growth, thirst, grasping, — these things belong to materialism, they are not mine. These are things that are the object of worldly interest, to be sensed, handled and tasted; these are the things that attract one, that bind one to the external world; these are the things that appear in the elements that make up the aggregates of personality where, owing to the procreative force of lust, there arise all kinds of disaster, birth, sorrow, lamentation, pain, despair, disease, old age, death. All these things concern worldly interests and enjoyment; they lie along the path of the philosophers, which is not the path of the Dharma. When the true egolessness of things and persons is understood, discrimination ceases to assert itself; the lower mind-system ceases to function; the various Bodhisattva stages are followed one after another; the Bodhisattva is able to utter his ten inexhaustible vows and is anointed by all the Buddhas. The Bodhisattva becomes master of himself and of all things by virtue of a life of spontaneous and radiant effortlessness. Thus the Dharma, which is Transcendental Intelligence, transcends all discriminations, all false-reasonings, all philosophical systems, all dualism.

*

THEN MAHAMATI SAID to the Blessed One: In the Scriptures mention is made of the Womb of Tathagatahood and it is taught that that which is born of it is by nature bright and pure, originally unspotted and endowed with the thirty-two marks of excellence. As it is described it is a precious gem but wrapped in a dirty garment soiled by greed, anger, folly and false-imagination. We are taught that this Buddha-nature immanent in every one is eternal, unchanging, auspicious. Is not this which is born of the

Womb of Tathagatahood the same as the soul-substance that is taught by the philosophers? The Divine Atman as taught by them is also claimed to be eternal, inscrutable, unchanging, imperishable. Is there, or is there not a difference?

The Blessed One replied: No, Mahamati, my Womb of Tathagatahood is not the same as the Divine Atman as taught by the philosophers. What I teach is Tathagatahood in the sense of Dharmakaya, Ultimate Oneness, Nirvana, emptiness, unbornness, unqualified-ness, devoid of will-effort. The reason why I teach the doctrine of Tathagatahood is to cause the ignorant and simple-minded to lay aside their fears as they listen to the teaching of egolessness and come to understand the state of non-discrimination and imagelessness. The religious teachings of the Tathagatas are just like a potter making various vessels by his own skill of hand with the aid of rod, water and thread, out of the one mass of clay, so the Tathagatas by their command of skillful means issuing from Noble Wisdom, by various terms, expressions, and symbols, preach the twofold egolessness in order to remove the last trace of discrimination that is preventing disciples from attaining a self-realisation of Noble Wisdom. The doctrine of the Tathagata-womb is disclosed in order to awaken philosophers from their clinging to the notion of a Divine Atman as transcendental personality, so that their minds that have become attached to the imaginary notion of "soul" as being something self-existent, may be quickly awakened to a state of perfect enlightenment. All such notions as causation, succession, atoms, primary elements, that make up personality, personal soul, Supreme Spirit, Sovereign God, Creator, are all figments of the imagination and manifestations of mind. No, Mahamati, the Tathagata's doctrine of the Womb of Tathagatahood is not the same as the philosopher's Atman.

The Bodhisattva is said to have well grasped the teachings of the Tathagatas when, all alone in a lonely place, by means of his Transcendental Intelligence, he walks the path leading to Nirvana. Thereon his mind will unfold by perceiving, thinking, meditating, and, abiding in the practise of concentration until he attains the "turning about" at the source of habit-energy, he will thereafter lead a life of excellent deeds. His mind concentrated on the state of Buddhahood, he will become thoroughly conversant with the noble truth of self-realisation; he will become perfect master of his own mind; he will be like a gem radiating many colors; he will be able to assume bodies of transformation; he will be able to enter into the minds of all to help them; and, finally, by gradually ascending the stages he will become established in the perfect Transcendental Intelligence of the Tathagatas.

Nevertheless, Transcendental Intelligence *(Aryajnana)* is not Noble Wisdom *(Arya-prajna)* itself; it is only an intuitive awareness of it. Noble Wisdom is a perfect state of imagelessness; it is the Womb of "Suchness"; it is the all-conserving Divine Mind *(Alayavijnana)* which in its pure Essence forever abides in perfect patience and undisturbed tranquility.

Chapter VII

Self–Realisation

THEN SAID MAHAMATI Pray tell us, Blessed One, what is the nature of self-realisation by reason of which we shall be able to attain Transcendental Intelligence?

The Blessed One replied: Transcendental Intelligence rises when the intellectual-mind reaches its limit and, if things are to be realised in their true and essence nature, its processes of mentation, which are based on particularised ideas, discriminations and judgments, must be transcended by an appeal to some higher faculty of cognition, if there be such a higher faculty. There is such a faculty in the intuitive-mind *(Manas)*, which as we have seen is the link between the intellectual-mind and Universal Mind. While it is not an individualised organ like the intellectual-mind, it has that which is much better, — direct dependence upon Universal Mind. While intuition does not give information that can be analysed and discriminated, it gives that which is far superior, — self-realisation through identification.

*

MAHAMATI THEN ASKED the Blessed One, saying: Pray tell us, Blessed One, what clear understandings an earnest disciple should have if he is to be successful in the discipline that leads to self-realisation?

The Blessed One replied: There are four things by the fulfilling of which an earnest disciple may gain self-realisation of Noble Wisdom and become a Bodhisattva-Mahasattva: First, he must have a clear understanding that all things are only manifestations of the mind itself; second, he must discard the notion of birth, abiding and disappearance; third, he must clearly understand the egolessness of both things and persons; and fourth, he must have a true conception of what constitutes self-realisation of Noble Wisdom. Provided with these four understandings, earnest disciples may become Bodhisattvas and attain Transcendental Intelligence.

As to the first; he must recognise and be fully convinced that this triple world is nothing but a complex manifestation of one's mental activities; that it is devoid of selfness and its belongings; that there are no strivings, no comings, no goings. He must recognise and accept the fact that this triple world is manifested and imagined as real only under the influence of habit-energy that has been accumulated since the beginning-less past by reason of memory, false-imagination, false-reasoning, and attachments to the multiplicities of objects and reactions in close relationship and in conformity to ideas of body-property-and-abode.

As to the second; he must recognise and be convinced that all things are to be regarded as forms seen in a vision and a dream, empty of substance, un-born and without self-nature; that all things exist only by reason of a complicated network of causation which owes its rise to discrimination and attachment and which eventuates in the rise of the mind-system and its belongings and evolvements.

As to the third; he must recognise and patiently accept the fact that his own mind and personality is also mind-constructed, that it is empty of substance, unborn and egoless. With these three things clearly in mind, the Bodhisattva will be able to enter into the truth of imagelessness.

As to the fourth; he must have a true conception of what constitutes self-realisation of Noble Wisdom. First, it is not comparable to the perceptions attained by the sense-mind, neither is it comparable to the cognition of the discriminating and intellectual-mind. Both of these presuppose a difference between self and not-self and the knowledge so attained is characterised by individuality and generality. Self-realisation is based on identity and oneness; there is nothing to be discriminated nor predicated concerning it. But to enter into it the Bodhisattva must be free from all presuppositions and attachments to things, ideas and selfness.

*

THEN SAID MAHAMATI to the Blessed One: Pray tell us, Blessed One, concerning the characteristics of deep attachments to existence and as to how we may become detached from existence?

The Blessed One replied: When one tries to understand the significance of things by means of words and discriminations, there follow immeasurably deep-seated attachments to existence. For instance: there are the deep-seated attachments to signs of individuality, to causation, to the notion of being and non-being, to the discrimination of birth and death, of doing and not-doing, to the habit of discrimination itself upon which the philosophers are so dependent.

There are three attachments that are especially deep-seated in the minds of all: greed, anger and infatuation, which are based on lust, fear and pride. Back of these lies discrimination and desire which is procreative and is accompanied with excitement and avariciousness and love of comfort and desire for eternal life; and, following, is a succession of rebirths on the five paths of existence and a continuation of attachments. But if these attachments are broken off, no signs of attachment nor of detachment will remain because they are based on things that are non-existent; when this truth is clearly understood the net of attachment is cleared away.

But depending upon and attaching itself to the triple combination which works in unison there is the rising and the continuation of the mind-system incessantly functioning, and because of it there is the deeply-felt and continuous assertion of the will-to-live. When the triple combination that causes the functioning of the mind-system ceases to exist, there is the triple emancipation and there is no further rising of any combination. When the existence and the non-existence of the external world are recognised as rising from the mind itself, then the Bodhisattva is prepared to enter into the state of imagelessness and therein to see into the emptiness which characterises all discrimination and all the deep-seated attachments resulting therefrom. Therein he will see no signs of deep-rooted attachment nor detachment; therein he will see no one in bondage and no one in emancipation, except those who themselves cherish bondage and emancipation, because in all things there is no "substance" to be taken hold of.

But so long as these discriminations are cherished by the ignorant and simple-minded they go on attaching themselves to them and, like the silkworm, go on spinning their thread of discrimination and enwrapping themselves and others, and are charmed with their prison. But to the wise there are no signs of attachment nor of detachment; all things are seen as abiding in solitude where there is no evolving of discrimination. Mahamati, you and all the Bodhisattvas should have your abode where you can see all things from the view-point of solitude.

Mahamati, when you and other Bodhisattvas understand well the distinction between attachment and detachment, you will be in possession of skillful means for avoiding becoming attached to words according to which one proceeds to grasp meanings. Free from the domination of words you will be able to establish yourselves where there will be a "turning about" in the deepest seat of consciousness by means of which you will attain self-realisation of Noble Wisdom and be able to enter into all the Buddha-lands and assemblies. There you will be stamped with the stamp of the powers, self-command, the psychic faculties, and will be endowed with the wisdom and the power of the ten inexhaustible vows, and will become radiant with the variegated rays of the Transformation Bodies. Therewith you will shine without effort like the moon, the sun, the magic wishing-jewel, and at every stage will view things as being of perfect oneness with yourself, uncontaminated by any self-consciousness. Seeing that all things are like a dream, you will be able to enter into the stage of the Tathagatas and be able to deliver discourses on the Dharma to the world of beings in accordance with their needs and be able to free them from all dualistic notions and false discriminations.

Mahamati, there are two ways of considering self-realisation: namely, the teachings about it, and the realisation itself. The teachings as variously given in the nine divisions of the doctrinal works, for the instructions of those who are inclined toward it, by making use of skillful means and expedients, are intended to awaken in all beings a true perception of the Dharma. The teachings are designed to keep one away from all the dualistic notions of being and non-being and oneness and otherness.

Realisation itself is within the inner consciousness. It is an inner experience that has no connection with the lower mind-system and its discriminations of words, ideas and philosophical speculations. It shines out with its own clear light to reveal the error and foolishness of mind-constructed teachings, to render impotent evil influences from without, and to guide one unerringly to the realm of the good non-outflowings. Mahamati, when the earnest disciple and Bodhisattva is provided with these requirements, the way is open to his perfect attainment of self-realisation of Noble Wisdom, and to the full enjoyment of the fruits that arise therefrom.

*

THEN MAHAMATI ASKED the Blessed One, saying: Pray tell us, Blessed One, about the One Vehicle which the Blessed One has said characterises the attainment of the inner self-realisation of Noble Wisdom?

The Blessed One replied: In order to discard more easily discriminations and erroneous reasonings, the Bodhisattva should retire by himself to a quiet, secluded place where he may reflect within himself without relying on anyone else, and there let him exert himself to make successive advances along the stages; this solitude is the characteristic feature of the inner attainment of self-realisation of Noble Wisdom.

I call this the One Vehicle, not because it is the One Vehicle, but because it is only in solitude that one is able to recognise and realise the path of the One Vehicle. So long as the mind is distracted and is making conscious effort, there can be no culmination as regards the various vehicles; it is only when the mind is alone and quiet that it is able to forsake the discriminations of the external world and seek realisation of an inner realm where there is neither vehicle nor one who rides in it. I speak of the three vehicles in order to carry the ignorant. I do not speak much about the One Vehicle because there is no way by which earnest disciples and masters can realise Nirvana, unaided. According to the discourses of the Tathagatas earnest disciples should be segregated and disciplined and trained in meditation and dhyana whereby they are aided by many devices and expedients to realise emancipation. It is because earnest disciples and masters have not fully destroyed the habit-energy of karma and the hindrances of discriminative knowledge and human passion that they are often unable to accept the twofold egolessness and the inconceivable transformation death, that I preach the triple vehicle and not the One Vehicle. When earnest disciples have gotten rid of all their evil habit-energy and been able to realise the twofold egolessness, then they will not be intoxicated by the bliss of the Samadhis and will be awakened into the super-realm of the good non-outflowings. Being awakened into the realm of the good non-outflowings, they will be able to gather up all the requisites for the attainment of Noble Wisdom which is beyond conception and is of sovereign power. But really, Mahamati, there are no vehicles, and so I speak of the One Vehicle. Mahamati, the full recognition of the One Vehicle has never been attained by either earnest disciples, masters, or even by the great Brahma; it has been attained only by the Tathagatas themselves. That is the reason that it is known as the One Vehicle. I do not speak much about it because there is no way by which earnest disciples can realise Nirvana unaided.

*

THEN MAHAMATI ASKED the Blessed One, saying: What are the steps that will lead an awakened disciple toward the self-realisation of Noble Wisdom?

The Blessed One replied: The beginning lies in the recognition that the external world is only a manifestation of the activities of the mind itself, and that the mind grasps it as an external world simply because of its habit of discrimination and false-reasoning. The disciple must get into the habit of looking at things truthfully. He must recognise the fact that the world has no self-nature, that it is un-born, that it is like a passing cloud, like an imaginary wheel made by a revolving firebrand, like the castle of the Gandharvas, like the moon reflected in the ocean, like a vision, a mirage, a dream. He must come to understand that mind in its essence-nature has nothing to do with discrimination nor causation; he must not listen to discourses based on the imaginary terms of qualifications; he must understand that Universal Mind in its pure essence is a state of imagelessness, that it is only because of the accumulated defilements on its face that body-property-and-abode appear to be its manifestations, that in its own pure nature it is unaffected and unaffecting by such changes as rising, abiding and destruction; he must fully understand that all these things come with the awakening of the notion of an ego-soul and its conscious mind. Therefore, Mahamati, let those disciples who wish to realise Noble Wisdom by following the Tathagata Vehicle desist from all discrimination and erroneous reasoning about such notions as the elements that make up the aggregates of personality and its sense-world or about such ideas as causation, rising, abiding and destruction, and exercise themselves in the discipline of dhyana that leads to the realisation of Noble Wisdom.

To practice dhyana, the earnest disciple should retire to a quiet and solitary place, remembering that life-long habits of discriminative thinking cannot be broken off easily nor quickly. There are four kinds of concentrative meditation *(dhyana):* The dhyana practised by the ignorant; the dhyana devoted to the examination of meaning; the dhyana with "suchness" *(tathata)* for its object; and the dhyana of the Tathagatas.

The dhyana practised by the ignorant is the one resorted to by those who are following the example of the disciples and masters but who do not understand its purpose and, therefore, it becomes "still-sitting" with vacant minds. This dhyana is practised, also, by those who, despising the body, see it as a shadow and a skeleton full of suffering and impurity, and yet who cling to the notion of an ego, seek to attain emancipation by the mere cessation of thought.

The dhyana devoted to the examination of meaning, is the one practised by those who, perceiving the untenability of such ideas as self, other and both, which are held by the philosophers, and who have passed beyond the twofold-egolessness, devote dhyana to an examination of the significance of egolessness and the differentiations of the Bodhisattva stages.

The dhyana with Tathata, or "Suchness," or Oneness, or the Divine Name, for its object is practised by those earnest disciples and masters who, while fully recognising the twofold egolessness and the imagelessness of Tathata, yet cling to the notion of an ultimate Tathata.

The dhyana of the Tathagatas is the dhyana of those who are entering upon the stage of Tathagatahood and who, abiding in the triple bliss which characterises the self-realisation of Noble Wisdom, are devoting themselves for the sake of all beings to the accomplishment of incomprehensible works for their emancipation. This is the pure dhyana of the Tathagatas. When all lesser things and ideas are transcended and forgotten, and there remains only a perfect state of imagelessness where Tathagata and Tathata are merged into perfect Oneness, then the Buddhas will come together from all their Buddha-lands and with shining hands resting on his forehead will welcome a new Tathagata.

Chapter VIII

THE ATTAINMENT OF SELF–REALISATION

THEN SAID MAHAMATI to the Blessed One: Pray tell us more as to what constitutes the state of self-realisation?

The Blessed One replied: In the life of an earnest disciple there are two aspects that are to be distinguished: namely, the state of attachment to the self-natures arising from discrimination of himself and his field of consciousness to which he is related; and second, the excellent and exalted state of self-realisation of Noble Wisdom. The state of attachment to the discriminations of the self-natures of things, ideas and selfhood is accompanied by emotions of pleasure or aversion according to experience or as laid down in books of logic. Conforming himself to the egolessness of things and holding back wrong views as to his own egoness, he should abandon these thoughts and hold himself firmly to the continuously ascending journey of the stages.

The exalted state of self-realisation as it relates to an earnest disciple is a state of mental concentration in which he seeks to identify himself with Noble Wisdom. In that effort he must seek to annihilate all vagrant thoughts and notions belonging to the externality of things, and all ideas of individuality and generality, of suffering and impermanence, and cultivate the noblest ideas of egolessness and emptiness and imagelessness; thus will he attain a realisation of truth that is free from passion and is ever serene. When this active effort at mental concentration is successful it is followed by a more passive, receptive state of Samadhi in which the earnest disciple will enter into the blissful abode of Noble Wisdom and experience its consummations in the transformations of Samapatti. This is an earnest disciple's first experience of the exalted state of realisation, but as yet there is no discarding of habit-energy nor escaping from the transformation of death.

Having attained this exalted and blissful state of realisation as far as it can be attained by disciples, the Bodhisattva must not give himself up to the enjoyment of its bliss, for that would mean cessation, but should think compassionately of other beings and keep ever fresh his original vows; he should never let himself rest in nor exert himself in the bliss of the Samadhis.

But, Mahamati, as earnest disciples go on trying to advance on the path that leads to full realisation, there is one danger against which they must be on their guard. Disciples may not appreciate that the mind-system, because of its accumulated habit-energy, goes on functioning, more or less unconsciously, as long as they live. They may sometimes think that they can expedite the attainment of their goal of tranquillisation by entirely suppressing the activities of the mind-system. This is a mistake, for even if the activities of the mind are suppressed, the mind will still go on functioning because the seeds of habit-energy will still remain in it. What they think is extinction of mind, is really the non-functioning of the mind's external world to which they are no longer attached. That is, the goal of tranquillisation is to be reached not by suppressing all mind activity but by getting rid of discriminations and attachments.

Then there are others who, afraid of the suffering incident to the discriminations of life and death, unwisely seek Nirvana. They have come to see that all things subject to discrimination have no reality and so imagine that Nirvana must consist in the annihilation of the senses and their fields of sensation; they do not appreciate that birth-and-death and Nirvana are not separate one from the other. They do not know that Nirvana is Universal Mind in its purity. Therefore, these stupid ones who cling to the notion that Nirvana is a world by itself that is outside what is seen by the mind, ignoring all the teachings of the Tathagatas concerning the external world, go on rolling themselves along the wheel of birth-and-death. But when they experience the "turning-about" in their deepest consciousness which will bring with it the perfect self-realisation of Noble Wisdom, then they will understand.

The true functioning of the mind is very subtle and difficult to be understood by young disciples, even masters with all their powers of right-knowledge and Samadhis often find it baffling. It is only the Tathagatas and the Bodhisattvas who are firmly established on the seventh stage who can fully understand its workings. Those earnest disciples and masters who wish to fully understand all the aspects of the different stages of Bodhisattvahood by the aid of their right-knowledge must do so by becoming thoroughly convinced that objects of discrimination are only seen to be so by the mind and, thus, by keeping themselves away from all discriminations and false reasonings which are also of the mind itself, by ever seeking to see things truly *(yathabhutam)*, and by planting roots of goodness in Buddha-lands that know no limits made by differentiations.

To do all this the Bodhisattva should keep himself away from all turmoil, social excitements and sleepiness; let him keep away from the treatises and writings of worldly philosophers, and from the ritual and ceremonies of professional priestcraft. Let him retire to a secluded place in the forest and there devote himself to the practise of the various spiritual disciplines, because it is only by so doing that he will become capable of attaining in this world of multiplicities a true insight into the workings of Universal Mind in its Essence. There surrounded by his good friends the Buddhas, earnest disciples will become capable of understanding the significance of the mind-system and its place as a mediating agent between the external world and Universal Mind and he will become capable of crossing the ocean of birth-and-death which rises from ignorance, desire and deed.

Having gained a thorough understanding of the mind-system, the three self-natures, the twofold egolessness, and established himself in the measure of self-realisation that goes with that attainment, all of which may be gained by his right-knowledge, the way will be clear for the Bodhisattva's further advance along the stages of Bodhisattvahood. The disciple should then abandon the understanding of mind which he has gained by right-knowledge, which in comparison with Noble Wisdom is like a lame donkey, and entering on the eighth stage of Bodhisattvahood, he should then discipline himself in Noble Wisdom according to its three aspects.

These aspects are: First, imagelessness which comes forth when all things belonging to discipleship, mastership, and philosophy are thoroughly mastered. Second, the power added by all the Buddhas by reason of their original vows including the identification of their lives and the sharing of their merit with all sentient lives. Third, the perfect self-realisation that thus far has only been realised in a measure. As the Bodhisattva succeeds in detaching himself from viewing all things, including his own imagined egoness, in their phenomenality, and realises the states of Samadhi and Samapatti whereby he surveys the world as a vision and a dream, and being sustained by all the Buddhas, he will be able to pass on to the full attainment of the Tathagata stage, which is Noble Wisdom itself. This is the triplicity of the noble life and being furnished with this triplicity the perfect self-realisation of Noble Wisdom has been attained.

*

THEN MAHAMATI ASKED the Blessed One, saying: Blessed One, is the purification of the evil outflowings of the mind which come from clinging to the notions of an objective world and an empirical soul, gradual or instantaneous?

The Blessed One replied: There are three characteristic out-flows of the mind, namely, the evil outflowings that rise from thirst, grasping and attachment; the evil out-flowings that arise from the illusions of the mind and the infatuations of egoism; and the good non-outflowings that arise from Noble Wisdom. The evil out-flowings that take place from recognising an external world, which in truth is only a manifestation of mind, and from becoming attached to it, are gradually purified and not instantaneously. Good behavior can only come by the path of restraint and effort. It is like a potter making pots that is done gradually and with attention and effort. It is like the mastery of comedy, dancing, singing, lute-playing, writing, and any other art; it must be acquired gradually and laboriously. Its reward will be a clearing insight into the emptiness and transiency of all things.

The evil out-flowings that arise from the illusions of the mind and the infatuations of egoism, concern the mental life more directly and are such things as fear, anger, hatred and pride; these are purified by study and meditation and that, too, must be attained gradually and not instantaneously. It is like the amra fruit that ripens

76

slowly; it is like grass, shrubs, herbs and trees that grow up from the earth gradually. Each must follow the path of study and meditation by himself gradually and with effort, but because of the original vows of the Bodhisattvas and all the Tathagatas who have devoted their merits and identified their lives with all animate life that all may be emancipated, they are not without aid and encouragement; but even with the aid of the Tathagatas, the purification of the evil out-flowings of the mind are at best slow and gradual, requiring both zeal and patience. Its reward is the gradual understanding of the twofold egolessness and its patient acceptance, and the feet well set on the stages of Bodhisattvahood.

But the good non-outflowings that come with self-realisation of Noble Wisdom, is a purification that comes instantaneously by the grace of the Tathagatas. It is like a mirror reflecting all forms and images instantaneously and without discrimination; it is like the sun or the moon revealing all forms instantaneously and illuminating them dispassionately with its light. In the same way the Tathagatas lead earnest disciples to a state of imagelessness; all the accumulations of habit-energy and karma that had been collecting since beginningless time because of attachment to erroneous views which have been entertained regarding an ego-soul and its external world, are cleared away, revealing instantaneously the realm of Transcendental Intelligence that belongs to Buddahood. Just as Universal Mind defiled by accumulations of habit-energy and karma reveals multiplicities of ego-souls and their external worlds of false-imagination, so Universal Mind cleared of its defilements through the gradual purifications of the evil out-flowings that come by effort, study and meditation, and by the gradual self-realisation of Noble Wisdom, at the long last, like the Dharmata Buddha shining forth spontaneously with the rays that issue from its pure Self-nature, shines forth instantaneously. By it the mentality of all Bodhisattvas is matured instantaneously: they find themselves in the palatial abodes of the Akanistha heavens, themselves spontaneously radiating the various treasures of its spiritual abundance.

Chapter IX

The Fruit of Self-Realisation

MAHAMATI ASKED the Blessed One: Pray tell us, Blessed One, what is the fruitage that comes with self-realisation of Noble Wisdom?

The Blessed One replied: First, there will come a clearing insight into the meaning and significance of things and following that will come an unfolding insight into the significance of the spiritual ideals *(Paramitas)* by reason of which the Bodhisattvas will be able to enter more deeply into the abode of imagelessness and be able to experience the higher Samadhis and gradually to pass through the higher stages of Bodhisattvahood.

After experiencing the "turning-about" in the deepest seat of consciousness, they will experience other Samadhis even to the highest, the Vajravimbopama, which belongs to the Tathagatas and their transformations. They will be able to enter into the realm of consciousness that lies beyond the consciousness of the mind-system, even the consciousness of Tathagatahood. They will become endowed with all the powers, psychic faculties, self-mastery, loving compassion, skillful means, and ability to enter into other Buddha-lands. Before they had attained self-realisation of Noble Wisdom they had been influenced by the self-interests of egoism, but after they attain self - realisation they will find themselves reacting spontaneously to the impulses of a great and compassionate heart endowed with skillful and boundless means and sincerely and wholly devoted to the emancipation of all beings.

*

MAHAMATI SAID: Blessed One, tell us about the sustaining power of the Tathagatas by which the Bodhisattvas are aided to attain self-realisation of Noble Wisdom?

The Blessed One replied: There are two kinds of sustaining power, which issue from the Tathagatas and are at the service of the Bodhisattvas, sustained by which the Bodhisattvas should prostrate themselves before them and show their appreciation by asking questions. The first kind of sustaining power is the Bodhisattva's own adoration and faith in the Buddhas by reason of which the Buddhas are able to manifest themselves and render their aid and to ordain them with their own hands. The second kind of sustaining power is the power radiating from the Tathagatas that enables the Bodhisattvas to attain and to pass through the various Samadhis and Samapattis without becoming intoxicated by their bliss.

Being sustained by the power of the Buddhas, the Bodhisattva even at the first stage will be able to attain the

Samadhi known as the Light of Mahayana. In that Samadhi Bodhisattvas will become conscious of the presence of the Tathagatas coming from all their different abodes in the ten quarters to impart to the Bodhisattvas their sustaining power in various ways. As the Bodhisattva Vajragarbha was sustained in his Samadhis and as many other Bodhisattvas of like degree and virtue have been sustained, so all earnest disciples and masters and Bodhisattvas may experience this sustaining power of the Buddhas in their Samadhis and Samapattis. The disciple's faith and the Tathagata's merit are two aspects of the same sustaining power and by it alone are the Bodhisattvas enabled to become one with the company of the Buddhas.

Whatever Samadhis, psychic faculties and teachings are realised by the Bodhisattvas, they are made possible only by the sustaining power of the Buddhas; if it were otherwise, the ignorant and the simpleminded might attain the same fruitage. Wherever the Tathagatas enter with their sustaining power there will be music, not only music made by human lips and played by human hands on various instruments, but there will be music among the grass and shrubs and trees, and in mountains and towns and palaces and hovels; much more will there be music in the hearts of those endowed with sentiency. The deaf, dumb and blind will be cured of their deficiencies and will rejoice in their emancipation. Such is the extraordinary virtue of the sustaining power imparted by the Tathagatas.

By the bestowal of this sustaining power, the Bodhisattvas are enabled to avoid the evils of passion, hatred and enslaving karma; they are enabled to transcend the dhyana of the beginners and to advance beyond the experience and truth already attained; they are enabled to demonstrate the Paramitas; and finally, to attain the stage of Tathagatahood. Mahamati, if it were not for this sustaining power, they would relapse into the ways and thoughts of the philosophers, easygoing disciples and the evil-minded, and would thus fall short of the highest attainment. For these reasons, earnest disciples and sincere Bodhisattvas are sustained by the power of all the Tathagatas.

*

THEN SAID MAHAMATI: It has been said by the Blessed One that by fulfilling the six Paramitas, Buddhahood is realised. Pray tell us what the Paramitas are, and how they are to be fulfilled?

The Blessed One replied: The Paramitas are ideals of spiritual perfection that are to be the guide of the Bodhisattvas on the path to self-realisation. There are six of them but they are to be considered in three different ways according to the progress of the Bodhisattva on the stages. At first they are to be considered as ideals for the worldly life; next as ideals for the mental life; and, lastly, as ideals of the spiritual and unitive life.

In the worldly life where one is still holding tenaciously to the notions of an ego-soul and what concerns it and holding fast to discriminations of dualism, if only for worldly benefits, one should cherish ideals of charity, good behavior, patience, zeal, thoughtfulness and wisdom. Even in the worldly life the practice of these virtues will bring rewards of happiness and success.

Much more in the mind-world of earnest disciples and masters will their practice bring joys of emancipation, enlightenment and peace of mind, because the Paramitas are grounded on right-knowledge and lead to thoughts of Nirvana, even if the Nirvana of their thoughts is for themselves. In the mind-world the Paramitas become more ideal and more sympathetic; charity can no longer be expressed in the giving of impersonal gifts but will call for the more costly gifts of sympathy and understanding; good behavior will call for something more than outward conformity to the five precepts because in the light of the Paramitas they must practise humility, simplicity, restraint and self-giving. Patience will call for something more than forbearance with external circumstances and the temperaments of other people: it will now call for patience with one's self. Zeal will call for something more than industry and outward show of earnestness: it will call for more self-control in the task of following the Noble Path and in manifestating the Dharma in one's own life. Thoughtfulness will give way to mindfulness wherein discriminated meanings and logical deductions and rationalisations will give way to intuitions of significance and spirit. The Paramita of Wisdom *(Prajna)* will no longer be concerned with pragmatic wisdom and erudition, but will reveal itself in its true perfectness of All-inclusive Truth which is Love.

The third aspect of the Paramitas as seen in the ideal perfections of the Tathagatas can only be fully understood by the Bodhisattva-Mahasattvas who are devoted to the highest spiritual discipline and have fully understood that there is nothing to be seen in the world but that which issues from the mind itself; in whose minds the discriminations of dualities has ceased to function; and seizing and clinging has become non-existent. Thus free from all attachments to individual objects and ideas, their minds are free to consider ways of benefitting and giving happiness to others, even to all sentient beings. To the Bodhisattva-Mahasattvas the ideal of charity is shown in the self-yielding of the Tathagata's hope of Nirvana that all may enjoy it together. While having relations with an objective world there is no rising in the minds of the Tathagatas of discriminations between the interests of self and the interests of others, between good and evil,—there is just the spontaneity and effortless actuality of perfect behavior. To practise patience with full knowledge of this and that, of grasp and grasping, but with no thought of discrimination nor of attachment,—that is the Tathagatas Paramita of Patience. To exert oneself with energy from the first part of the night to its end in conformity with the disciplinary measures with no rising of discrimination as to comfort or discomfort,— that is the Tathagata's Paramita of Zeal. Not to discriminate between self and others in thoughts of Nirvana, but to keep the mind fixed on Nirvana,—that is the Paramita of Mindfulness. As to the Prajna-Paramita, which is Noble Wisdom, who can predicate it? When in Samadhi the mind ceases to discriminate and there is only perfect and love-filled imagelessness, then an inscrutable "turning-about" will take place in the inmost consciousness and one will have attained self-realisation of Noble Wisdom, — that is the highest Prajna-Paramita.

*

THEN MAHAMATI SAID to the Blessed One: You have spoken of an astral-body, a "mind-vision-body" (*manomayakaya*) which the Bodhisattvas are able to assume, as being one of the fruits of self-realisation of Noble Wisdom: pray tell us, Blessed One, what is meant by such a transcendental body?

The Blessed One replied: There are three kinds of such transcendental bodies: First, there is the one in which the Bodhisattva attains enjoyment of the Samadhis and Samapattis. Second, there is the one which is assumed by the Tathagatas according to the class of beings to be sustained, and which achieves and perfects spontaneously with no attachment and no effort. Third, there is the one in which the Tathagatas receive their intuition of Dharmakaya.

The transcendental personality that enters into the enjoyment of the Samadhis comes with the third, fourth and fifth stages as the mentations of the mind-system become quieted and waves of consciousness are no more stirred on the face of Universal Mind. In this state, the conscious-mind is still aware, in a measure, of the bliss being experienced by this cessation of the mind's activities.

The second kind of transcendental personality is the kind assumed by the Bodhisattvas and Tathagatas as bodies of transformation by which they demonstrate their original vows in the work of achieving and perfecting; it comes with the eighth stage of Bodhisattvahood. When the Bodhisattva has a thorough-going penetration into the maya-like nature of things and understands the dharma of imagelessness, he will experience the "turning-about" in his deepest consciousness and will become able to experience the higher Samadhis even to the highest. By entering into these exalted Samadhis he attains a personality that transcends the conscious-mind, by reason of which he obtains supernatural powers of self-mastery and activities because of which he is able to move as he wishes, as quickly as a dream changes, as quickly as an image changes in a mirror. This transcendental body is not a product of the elements and yet there is something in it that is analogous to what is so produced; it is furnished with all the differences appertaining to the world of form but without their limitations; possessed of this "mind-vision-body" he is able to be present in all the assemblages in all the Buddha-lands. Just as his thoughts move instantly and without hindrance over walls and rivers and trees and mountains, and just as in memory he recalls and visits the scenes of his past experiences, so, while his mind keeps functioning in the body, his thoughts may be a hundred thousand yojanas away. In the same fashion the transcendental personality that experiences the Samadhi Vajravimbopama will be endowed with supernatural powers and psychic faculties and self-mastery by reason of which he will be able to follow the noble paths that lead to the assemblages of the Buddhas, moving about as freely as he may wish. But his wishes will no longer be self-centered nor tainted by discrimination and attachment, for this transcendental personality is not his old body, but is the transcendental embodiment of his original vows of self-yielding in order to bring all beings to maturity.

The third kind of transcendental personality is so ineffable that it is able to attain intuitions of the Dharmakaya, that is, it attains intuitions of the boundless and inscrutable cognition of Universal Mind. As Bodhisattva-Mahasattvas attain the highest of the stages and become conversant with all the treasures to be realised in Noble Wisdom, they will attain this inconceivable transformation-body which is the true nature of all the Tathagatas past, present and future, and will participate in the blissful peace which pervades the Dharma of all the Buddhas.

Chapter X

DISCIPLESHIP: LINEAGE OF THE ARHATS

THEN MAHAMATI ASKED the Blessed One: Pray tell us how many kinds of disciples there are?

The Blessed One replied: There are as many kinds of disciples as there are individuals, but for convenience they may be divided into two groups: disciples of the lineage of the Arhats, and disciples known as Bodhisattvas. Disciples of the lineage of the Arhats may be considered under two aspects: First, according to the number of times they will return to this life of birth-and-death; and second, according to their spiritual progress. Under the first aspect, they may be subdivided into three groups: The "Stream-entered," the "Once-returning," and the "Never-returning."

The Stream-entered are those disciples, who having freed themselves from the attachments to the lower discriminations and who have cleansed themselves from the twofold hindrances and who clearly understand the meaning of the twofold egolessness, yet who still cling to the notions of individuality and generality and to their own egoness. They will advance along the stages to the sixth only to succumb to the entrancing bliss of the Samadhis.

They will be reborn seven times, or five times, or three times, before they will be able to pass the sixth stage. The Once-returning are the Arhats, and the Never-returning are the Bodhisattvas who have reached the seventh stage.

The reason for these gradations is because of their attachment to the three degrees of false-imagination: namely, faith in moral practices, doubt, and the view of their individual personality. When these three hindrances are overcome, they will be able to attain the higher stages. As to moral practices: the ignorant, simple-minded disciples obey the rules of morality, piety and penance, because they desire thereby to gain worldly advancement and happiness, with the added hope of being reborn in more favorable conditions. The Stream-entered ones do not cling to moral practices for any hope of reward for their minds are fixed on the exalted state of self-realisation; the reason they devote themselves to the details of morality is that they wish to master such truths as are in conformity with the undefiled out-flowings. As regards the hindrance of doubt in the Buddha's teachings, that will continue so long as any of the notions of discriminations are cherished and will disappear when they disappear. Attachment to the view of individual personality will be gotten rid of as the disciple gains a more thorough understanding of the notions of being and non-being, self-nature and egolessness, thereby getting rid of the attachments to his own selfness that goes with those discriminations. By breaking up and clearing away these three hindrances the

Stream-entered ones will be able to discard all greed, anger and folly.

As for the Once-returning Arhats; there was once in them the discrimination of forms, signs, and appearances, but as they gradually learned by right knowledge not to view individual objects under the aspect of quality and qualifying, and as they became acquainted with what marks the attainment of the practice of dhyana, they have reached a stage of enlightenment where in one more rebirth they will be able to put an end to the clinging to their own self-interests. Free of this burden of error and its attachments, the passions will no more assert themselves and the hindrances will be cleared away forever.

Under the second aspect disciples may be grouped according to the spiritual progress they have attained, into four classes, namely, disciples *(sravaka)*, masters *(pratyekabuddha)*, Arhats, and Bodhisattvas.

The first class of disciples mean well but they find it difficult to understand unfamiliar ideas. Their minds are joyful when studying about and practising the things belonging to appearances that can be discriminated, but they become confused by the notion of an uninterrupted chain of causation, and they become fearful when they consider the aggregates that make up personality and its object world as being maya-like, empty and egoless. They are able to advance to the fifth or sixth stage where they are able to do away with the rising of passions, but not with the notions that give rise to passion and, therefore, they are unable to get rid of the clinging to an ego-soul and its accompaning attachments, habits and habit-energy. In this same class of disciples are the earnest disciples of other faiths, who clinging to the notions of such things as, the soul as an eternal entity, Supreme Atman, Personal God, seek a Nirvana that is in harmony with them. There are others, more materialistic in their ideas, who think that all things exist in dependence upon causation and, therefore, that Nirvana must be in like dependence. But none of these, earnest though they be, have gained an insight into the truth of the twofold egolessness and are, therefore, of limited spiritual insight as regards deliverance and non-deliverance; for them there is no emancipation. They have great self-confidence but they can never gain a true knowledge of Nirvana until they have learned to discipline themselves in the patient acceptance of the twofold egolessness.

The second class of masters are those who have gained a high degree of intellectual understanding of the truths concerning the aggregates that make up personality and its external world but who are filled with fear when they face the significance and consequences of these truths, and the demands which their learning makes upon them, that is, not to become attached to the external world and its manifold forms making for comfort and power, and to keep away from the entanglements of its social relations. They are attracted by the possibilities that are attainable by so doing, namely, the possession of miraculous powers such as dividing the personality and appearing in different places at the same time, or manifesting bodies of transformation. To gain these powers they even resort to the solitary life, but this class of masters never get beyond the seductions of their learning and egoism, and their discourses are always in conformity with that characteristic and limitation. Among them are many earnest disciples who show a degree of spiritual insight that is characterised by sincerity and undismayed willingness to meet all the demands that the stages make upon them. When they see that all that makes up the objective world is only manifestation of mind, that it is without self-nature, un-born and egoless, they accept it without fear, and when they see that their own ego-soul is also empty, un-born and egoless, they are untroubled and undismayed, with earnest purpose they seek to adjust their lives to the full demands of these truths, but they cannot forget the notions that lie back of these facts, especially the notion of their own conscious ego-self and its relation to Nirvana. They are of the Stream-entered class.

The class known as Arhats are those earnest masters who belong to the once-returning class. By their spiritual insight they have reached the sixth and seventh stages. They have thoroughly understood the truth of the twofold egolessness and the imagelessness of Reality; with them there is no more discrimination, nor passions, nor pride of egoism; they have gained an exalted insight and seen into the immensity of the Buddha-lands. By attaining an inner perception of the true nature of Universal Mind they are steadily purifying their habit-energy. The Arhat has attained emancipation, enlightenment, the Dhyanas, the

Samadhis, and his whole attention is given to the attainment of Nirvana, but the idea of Nirvana causes mental perturbations because he has a wrong idea of Nirvana. The notion of Nirvana in his mind is divided: he discriminates Nirvana from self, and self from others. He has attained some of the fruits of self-realisation but he still thinks and discourses on the Dhyanas, subjects for meditation, the Samadhis, the fruits. He pridefully says: "There are fetters, but I am disengaged from them." His is a double fault: he both denounces the vices of the ego, and still clings to its fetters. So long as he continues to discriminate notions of dhyana, dhyana practice, subjects for dhyana, right-knowledge and truth, there is a bewildered state of mind,—he has not attained perfect emancipation. Emancipation comes with the acceptance of imagelessness.

He is master of the Dhyanas and enters into the Samadhis, but to reach the higher stages one must pass beyond the Dhyanas, the immeasurables, the world of no-form, and the bliss of the Samadhis into the Samapattis leading to the cessation of thought itself. The dhyana-practiser, dhyana, the subject of dhyana, the cessation of thought, once-returning, never-returning, all these are divided and bewildering states of mind. Not until all discrimination is abandoned is there perfect emancipation. Thus the Arhat, master of the dhyanas, participating in the Samadhis, but unsupported by the Buddhas yields to the entrancing bliss of the Samadhis—and passes to his Nirvana. The Arhat is in the class of the Once-returning.

Disciples and masters and Arhats may ascend the stages up to the sixth. They perceive that the triple world is no more than mind itself; they perceive that there is no becoming attached to the multiplicities of external objects except through the discriminations and activities of the mind itself; they perceive that there is no ego-soul; and, therefore, they attain a measure of tranquillisation. But their tranquillisation is not perfect every minute of their lives, for with them there is something effect-producing, some grasped and grasping, some lingering trace of dualism and egoism. Though disengaged from the actively functioning passions, they are still bound in with the habit-energy of passion and, becoming intoxicated with the wine of the Samadhis, they still have their abode in the realm of the out-flowings. Perfect tranquillisation is possible only with the seventh stage. So long as their minds are in confusion, they cannot attain to a clear conviction as to the cessation of all multiplicity and the actuality of the perfect oneness of all things. In their minds the self-nature of things is still discriminated as good and bad, therefore, their minds are in confusion and they cannot pass beyond the sixth stage. But at the sixth stage all discrimination ceases as they become engrossed in the bliss of the Samadhis wherein they cherish the thought of Nirvana and, as Nirvana is possible at the sixth stage, they pass into their Nirvana, but it is not the Nirvana of the Buddhas.

Chapter XI

BODHISATTVAHOOD AND ITS STAGES

THEN SAID MAHAMATI to the Blessed One: Will you tell us now about the disciples who are Bodhisattvas?

The Blessed One replied: The Bodhisattvas are those earnest disciples who are enlightened by reason of their efforts to attain self-realisation of Noble Wisdom and who have taken upon themselves the task to enlighten others. They have gained a clear understanding of the truth that all things are empty, un-born, and of a maya-like nature; they have ceased from viewing things discriminatively and from considering them in their relations; they thoroughly understand the truth of twofold egolessness and have adjusted themselves to it with patient acceptance; they have attained a definite realisation of imagelessness; and they are abiding in the perfect-knowledge that they have gained by self-realisation of Noble Wisdom.

Well stamped by the seal of "Suchness" they entered upon the first of the Bodhisattva stages. The first stage is called the Stage of Joy (Pramudita). Entering this stage is like passing out of the glare and shadows into a realm of "no-shadows"; it is like passing out of the noise and tumult of the crowded city into the quietness of solitude. The Bodhisattva feels within himself the awakening of a great heart of compassion and he utters his ten original vows: To honor and serve all Buddhas; to spread the knowledge and practice of the Dharma; to welcome all coming Buddhas; to practise the six Paramitas; to persuade all beings to embrace the Dharma; to attain a perfect understanding of the universe; to attain a perfect understanding of the mutuality of all beings; to attain perfect self -realisation of the oneness of all the Buddhas and Tathagatas in self-nature, purpose and resources; to become acquainted with all skillful means for the carrying out of these vows for the emancipation of all beings; to realise supreme enlightenment through the perfect self-realisation of Noble Wisdom, ascending the Stages and entering Tathagatahood.

In the spirit of these vows the Bodhisattva gradually ascends the stages to the sixth. All earnest disciples, masters and Arhats have ascended thus far, but being enchanted by the bliss of the Samadhis and not being supported by the powers of the Buddhas, they pass to their Nirvana. The same fate would befall the Bodhisattvas except for the sustaining power of the Buddhas, by that they are enabled to refuse to enter Nirvana until all beings can enter Nirvana with them. The Tathagatas point out to them the virtues of Buddahood which are beyond the conception of the intellectual-mind, and they encourage and strengthen the Bodhisattvas not to give in to the enchantment of the bliss of the Samadhis, but to press on to further advancement along the stages. If the Bodhisattvas had entered Nirvana at this stage, and they would have done so without the sustaining power of the Buddhas, there would have been the cessation of all things and the family of the Tathagatas would have become extinct.

Strengthened by the new strength that comes to them from the Buddhas and with the more perfect insight that is theirs by reason of their advance in self-realisation of Noble Wisdom, they re-examine the nature of the mind-system, the egolessness of personality, and the part that grasping and attachment and habit-energy play in the unfolding drama of life; they re-examine the illusions of the fourfold logical analysis, and the various elements that enter into enlightenment and self-realisation, and, in the thrill of their new powers of self-mastery, the Bodhisattvas enter upon the seventh stage of Far-going *(Duramgama).*

Supported by the sustaining power of the Buddhas, the Bodhisattvas at this stage enter into the bliss of the Samadhi of perfect tranquillisation. Owing to their original vows they are transported by emotions of love and compassion as they become aware of the part they are to perform in the carrying out of their vows for the emancipation of all beings. Thus they do not enter into Nirvana, but, in truth, they too are already in Nirvana because in their emotions of love and compassion there is no rising of discrimination; henceforth, with them, discrimination no more takes place. Because of Transcendental Intelligence only one conception is present—the promotion of the realisation of Noble

Wisdom. Their insight issues from the Womb of Tathagatahood and they enter into their task with spontaneity and radiancy because it is of the self-nature of Noble Wisdom. This is called the Bodhisattva's Nirvana — the losing oneself in the bliss of perfect self-yielding. This is the seventh stage, the stage of Far-going.

The eighth stage, is the stage of No-recession *(Acala)*. Up to this stage, because of the defilements upon the face of Universal Mind caused by the accumulation of habit-energy since beginningless time, the mind-system and all that pertains to it has been evolved and sustained. The mind-system functioned by the discriminations of an external and objective world to which it became attached and by which it was perpetuated. But with the Bodhisattva's attainment of the eighth stage there comes the "turning-about" within his deepest consciousness from self-centered egoism to universal compassion for all beings, by which he attains perfect self-realisation of Noble Wisdom. There is an instant cessation of the delusive activities of the whole mind-system; the dancing of the waves of habit-energy on the face of Universal Mind are forever stilled, revealing its own inherent quietness and solitude, the inconceivable Oneness of the Womb of Tathagatahood.

Henceforth there is no more looking outward upon an external world by senses and sense-minds, nor a discrimination of particularised concepts and ideas and propositions by an intellectual-mind, no more grasping, nor attachment, nor pride of egoism, nor habit-energy.

Henceforth there is only the inner experience of Noble Wisdom which has been attained by entering into its perfect Oneness.

Thus establishing himself at the eighth stage of No-recession, the Bodhisattva enters into the bliss of the ten Samadhis, but avoiding the path of the disciples and masters who yielded themselves up to their entrancing bliss and who passed to their Nirvanas, and supported by his vows and the Transcendental Intelligence which now is his and being sustained by the power of the Buddhas, he enters upon the higher paths that lead to Tathagatahood. He passes through the bliss of the Samadhis to assume the transformation body of a Tathagata that through him all beings may be emancipated. Mahamati, If there had been no Tathagata-womb and no Divine Mind then there would have been no rising and disappearance of the aggregates that make up personality and its external world, no rising and disappearance of ignorant people nor holy people, and no task for Bodhisattvas; therefore, while walking in the path of self-realisation and entering into the enjoyments of the Samadhis, you must never abandon working hard for the emancipation of all beings and your self-yielding love will never be in vain. To philosophers the conception of Tathagata-womb seems devoid of purity and soiled by these external manifestations, but it is not so understood by the Tathagatas,—to them it is not a proposition of philosophy but is an intuitive experience as real as though it was an amalaka fruit held in the palm of the hand.

With the cessation of the mind-system and all its evolving discriminations, there is cessation of all strain and effort. It is like a man in a dream who imagines he is crossing a river and who exerts himself to the utmost to do so, who is suddenly awakened. Being awake, he thinks: "Is this real or is it unreal?" Being now enlightened, he knows that it is neither real nor unreal. Thus when the Bodhisattva arrives at the eighth stage, he is able to see all things truthfully and, more than that, he is able to thoroughly understand the significance of all the dream-like things of his life as to how they came to pass and as to how they pass away. Ever since beginningless time the mind-system has perceived multiplicities of forms and conditions and ideas which the thinking-mind has discriminated and the empirical-mind has experienced and grasped and clung to. From this has risen habit-energy that by its accumulation has conditioned the illusions of existence and non-existence, individuality and generality, and has thus perpetuated the dream-state of false-imagination. But now, to the Bodhisattvas of the eighth stage, life is past and is remembered as it truly was—a passing dream.

As long as the Bodhisattva had not passed the seventh stage, even though he had attained an intuitive understanding of the true meaning of life and its maya-like nature, and as to how the mind carried on its discriminations and attachments yet, nevertheless, the cherishing of the notions of these things had continued and, although he no longer experienced within himself any ardent desire for things nor any impulse to grasp them yet, nevertheless, the notions concerning them persisted and perfumed his efforts to practise the teachings of the Buddhas and to labor for the emancipation of all beings. Now, in the eighth stage, even the notions have passed away, and all effort and striving is seen to be unnecessary. The Bodhisattva's Nirvana is perfect tranquillisation, but it is not extinction nor inertness; while there is an entire absence of discrimination and purpose, there is the freedom and spontaneity of potentiality that has come with the attainment and patient acceptance of the truths of egolessness and imagelessness. Here is perfect solitude, undisturbed by any gradation or continuous succession, but radiant with the potency and freedom of its self-nature which is the self-nature of Noble Wisdom, blissfully peaceful with the serenity of Perfect Love.

Entering upon the eighth stage, with the "turning-about" at the deepest seat of consciousness, the Bodhisattva will become conscious that he has received the second kind of Transcendental-body *(Manomayakaya)*. The transition from mortal-body to Transcendental-body has nothing to do with mortal death, for the old body continues to function and the old mind serves the needs of the old body, but now it is free from the control of mortal mind. There has been an inconceivable transformation-death *(acintya-parinama-cyuti)* by which the false-imagination of his particularised individual personality has been transcended by a realisation of his oneness with the universalised mind of Tathagatahood, from which realisation there will be no recession. With that realisation he finds himself amply endowed with all the Tathagata's powers, psychic faculties, and self-mastery, and, just as the good earth is the support of all beings in the world of desire *(karmadhatu)*, so the Tathagatas become the support of all beings in the Transcendental World of No-form.

The first seven of the Bodhisattva stages were in the realm of mind and the eighth, while transcending mind, was still in touch with it; but in the ninth stage of Transcendental Intelligence *(Sadhumati)*, by reason of his perfect intelligence and insight into the imagelessness of Divine Mind which he had attained by self-realisation of Noble Wisdom, he is in the realm of Tathagatahood. Gradually the Bodhisattva will realise his Tathagata-nature and the possession of all its powers and psychic faculties, self-mastery, loving compassion, and skillful means, and by means of them will enter into all the Buddha-lands. Making use of these new powers, the Bodhisattva will assume various transformation-bodies and personalities for the sake of benefiting others. Just as in the former mental life, imagination had risen from relative-knowledge, so now skillful-means rise spontaneously from Transcendental Intelligence. It is like the magical gem that reflects instantaneously appropriate responses to one's wishes. The Bodhisattva passes over to all the assemblages of the Buddhas and listens to them as they discourse on the dream-like nature of all things and concerning the truths that transcend all notions of being and non-being, that have no relation to birth and death, nor to eternality nor extinction. Thus facing the Tathagatas as they discourse on

Noble Wisdom that is far beyond the mental capacity of disciples and masters, he will attain a hundred thousand Samadhis, indeed, a hundred thousand nyutas of kotis of Samadhis, and in the spirit of these Samadhis he will instantly pass from one Buddha-land to another, paying homage to all the Buddhas, being born into all the celestial mansions, manifesting Buddha-bodies, and himself discoursing on the Triple Treasure to lesser Bodhisattvas that they too may partake of the fruits of self-realisation of Noble Wisdom.

Thus passing beyond the last stage of Bodhisattvahood, he becomes a Tathagata himself endowed with all the freedom of the Dharmakaya. The tenth stage belongs to the Tathagatas. Here the Bodhisattva will find himself seated upon a lotus-like throne in a splendid jewel-adorned palace and surrounded by Bodhisattvas of equal rank. Buddhas from all the Buddha-lands will gather about him and with their pure and fragrant hands resting on his forehead will give him ordination and recognition as one of themselves. Then they will assign him a Buddha-land that he may possess and perfect as his own.

The tenth stage is called the Great Truth Cloud *(Dharmamegha)*, inconceivable, inscrutable. Only the Tathagatas can realise its perfect Imagelessness and Oneness and Solitude. It is Mahesvara, the Radiant Land, the Pure Land, the Land of Far-distances; surrounding and surpassing the lesser worlds of form and desire *(karmadhatu)*, in which the Bodhisattva will find himself at-one-ment. Its rays of Noble Wisdom which is the self-nature of the Tathagatas, many-colored, entrancing, auspicious, are transforming the triple world as other worlds have been transformed in the past, and still other worlds will be transformed in the future. But in the Perfect Oneness of Noble Wisdom there is no gradation nor succession nor effort. The tenth stage is the first, the first is the eighth, the eighth is the fifth, the fifth is the seventh: what gradation can there be where perfect Imagelessness and Oneness prevail? And what is the reality of Noble Wisdom? It is the ineffable potency of the Dharmakaya; it has no bounds nor limits; it surpasses all the Buddhalands, and pervades the Akanistha and the heavenly mansions of the Tushita.

Chapter XII

TATHAGATAHOOD WHICH IS NOBLE WISDOM

THEN SAID MAHAMATI to the Blessed One: It has been taught in the canonical books that the Buddhas are subject to neither birth nor destruction, and you have said that "the Unborn" is one of the names of the Tathagatas; does that mean that the Tathagata is a non-entity?

The Blessed One replied: The Tathagata is not a non-entity nor is he to be conceived as other things are as neither born nor disappearing, nor is he subject to causation, nor is he without significance; yet I refer to him as "The Un-born." There is yet another name for the Tathagata, "The Mind-appearing One" *(Manomayakaya)* which his Essence-body assumes at will in the transformations incident to his work of emancipation. This is beyond the understanding of common disciples and masters and even beyond the full comprehension of those Bodhisattvas who remain in the seventh stage. Yes, Mahamati, "The Un-born" is synonymous with Tathagata.

Then Mahamati said: If the Tathagatas are un-born, there does not seem to be anything to take hold of—no entity—or is there something that bears another name than entity? And what can that "something" be?

The Blessed One replied: Objects are frequently known by different names according to different aspects that they present,—the god Indra is sometimes known as Shakra, and sometimes as Purandara. These different names are sometimes used interchangeably and sometimes they are discriminated, but different objects are not to be imagined because of the different names, nor are they without individuation. The same can be said of myself as I appear in this world of patience before ignorant people and where I am known by uncounted trillions of names. They address me by different names not realising that they are all names of the one Tathagata. Some recognise me as Tathagata, some as The Self-existent One, some as Gautama the Ascetic, some as Buddha. Then there are others who recognise me as Brahma, as Vishnu, as Ishvara; some see me as Sun, as Moon; some as a reincarnation of the ancient sages; some as one of "the ten powers"; some as Rama, some as Indra, and some as Varuna. Still there are others who speak of me as The Un-born, as Emptiness, as "Suchness," as Truth, as Reality, as Ultimate Principle; still there are others who see me as Dharmakaya, as Nirvana, as the Eternal; some speak of me as sameness, as non-duality, as undying, as formless; some think of me as the doctrine of Buddha-causation, or of Emancipation, or of the Noble Path; and some think of me as Divine Mind and Noble Wisdom. Thus in this world and in other worlds am I known by these uncounted names, but they all see me as the moon is seen in water. Though they all honor, praise and esteem me, they do not fully understand the meaning and significance of the words they use; not having their own self-realisation of Truth they cling to the words of their canonical books, or to what has been told them, or to what they have imagined, and fail to see that the name they are using is only one of the many names of the Tathagata. In their studies they follow the mere words of the text vainly trying to gain the true meaning, instead of having confidence in the one 'text" where self-confirming Truth is revealed, that is, having confidence in the self-realisation of Noble Wisdom.

THEN SAID MAHAMATI Pray tell us, Blessed One, about the self-nature of the Tathagatas?

The Blessed One replied: If the Tathagata is to be described by such expressions as made or un-made, effect or cause, we would have to describe him as neither made, nor un-made, nor effect, nor cause; but if we so described him we would be guilty of dualistic discrimination. If the Tathagata is something made, he would be impermanent; if he is impermanent anything made would be a Tathagata. If he is something un-made, then all effort to realise Tathagatahood would be useless. That which is neither an effect nor a cause, is neither a being nor a non-being, and that which is neither a being nor a non-being is outside the four propositions. The four propositions belong to worldly usage; that which is outside them is no more than a word, like a barren-woman's child; so are all the terms concerning the Tathagata to be understood.

When it is said that all things are egoless, it means that all things are devoid of self-hood. Each thing may have its own individuality—the being of a horse is not of cow nature—it is such as it is of its own nature and is thus discriminated by the ignorant, but, nevertheless, its own nature is of the nature of a dream or a vision. That is why the ignorant and the simple-minded, who are in the habit of discriminating appearances, fail to understand the significance of egolessness. It is not until discrimination is gotten rid of that the fact that all things are empty, un-born and without self-nature can be appreciated.

Mahamati, all these expressions as applied to the Tathagatas are without meaning, for that which is none of these is something removed from all measurement, and that which is removed from all measurement turns into a meaningless word; that which is a mere word is something un-born; that which is unborn is not subject to destruction; that which is not subject to destruction is like space and space is neither effect nor cause; that which is neither effect nor cause is something unconditioned; that which is unconditioned is beyond all reasoning; that which is beyond all reasoning,—that is the Tathagata. The self-nature of Tathagatahood is far removed from all predicates and measurements; the self-nature of Tathagatahood is Noble Wisdom.

*

THEN MAHAMATI SAID to the Blessed One: Are the Tathagatas permanent or impermanent?

The Blessed One replied: The Tathagatas are neither permanent nor impermanent; if either is asserted there is error connected with it. If the Tathagata is said to be permanent then he will be connected with the creating agencies for, according to the philosophers, the creating agencies are something uncreated and permanent. But the Tathagatas are not connected with the so-called creating agencies and in that sense he is impermanent. If he is said to be impermanent then he is connected with things that are created for they also are impermanent. For these reasons the Tathagatas are neither permanent nor impermanent.

Neither can the Tathagatas he said to be permanent in the sense that space is said to be permanent, or that the horns of a hare can be said to be permanent for, being unreal, they exclude all ideas of permanency or impermanency. This does not apply to the Tathagatas because they come forth from the habit-energy of ignorance which is connected with the mind-system and the elements that make up personality. The triple world originates from the discrimination of unrealities and where discrimination takes place there is duality and the notion of permanency and impermanency, but the Tathagatas do not rise from the discrimination of unrealities. Thus, as long as there is discrimination there will be the notion of permanency and impermanency; when discrimination is done away with, Noble Wisdom, which is based on the significance of solitude, will be established.

However, there is another sense in which the Tathagatas may be said to be permanent. Transcendental Intelligence rising with the attainment of enlightenment is of a permanent nature. This Truth-essence which is discoverable in the enlightenment of all who are enlightened, is realisable as the regulative and sustaining principle of Reality, which forever abides. The Transcendental Intelligence attained intuitively by the Tathagatas by their self-realisation of Noble Wisdom, is a realisation of their own self-nature,—in this sense the Tathagatas are permanent. The eternal-unthinkable of the Tathagatas is the "suchness" of Noble Wisdom realised within themselves. It is both eternal and beyond thought. It conforms to the idea of a cause and yet is beyond existence and non-existence. Because it is the exalted state of Noble-Wisdom, it has its own character. Because it is the cause of highest Reality, it is its own causation. Its eternality is not derived from reasonings based on external notions of being and non-being, nor of eternality nor non-eternality. Being classed under the same head as space, cessasion, Nirvana, it is eternal. Because it has nothing to do with existence and non-existence, it is no creator; because it has nothing to do with creation, nor with being and non-being, but is only revealed in the exalted state of Noble Wisdom, it is truly eternal.

When the twofold passions are destroyed, and the twofold hindrances are cleared away, and the twofold egolessness is fully understood, and the inconceivable transformation death of the Bodhisattva is attained— that which remains is the self-nature of the Tathagatas. When the teachings of the Dharma are fully understood and are perfectly realised by the disciples and masters, that which is realised in their deepest consciousness is their own Buddha-nature revealed as Tathagata.

In a true sense there are four kinds of sameness relating to Buddha-nature: there is sameness of letters, sameness of words, sameness of meaning, and sameness of Essence. The name Buddha is spelt: B-U-D-D-H-A; the letters are the same when used for any Buddha or Tathagata. When the Brahmans teach they use various words, and when the Tathagatas teach they use the very same words; in respect to words there is a sameness between us. In the teachings of all the Tathagatas there is a sameness of meaning. Among all the Buddhas there is a sameness of Buddha-nature. They all have the thirty-two marks of excellence and the eighty minor signs of bodily perfection; there is no distinction among them except as they manifest various transformations according to the different dispositions of beings who are to be disciplined and emancipated by various means. In the Ultimate Essence which is Dharmakaya, all the Buddhas of the past, present and future, are of one sameness.

*

THEN SAID MAHAMATI to the Blessed One: It has been said by the Blessed One that from the night of the Enlightenment to the night of the Parinirvana, the Tathagata has uttered no word nor ever will utter a word. In what deep meaning is this true?

The Blessed One replied: By two reasons of deepest meaning is it true: In the light of the Truth self-realised by Noble Wisdom; and in the Truth of an eternally-abiding Reality. The self-realisation of Noble Wisdom by all the Tathagatas is the same as my own self-realisation of Noble Wisdom; there is no more, no less, no difference; and all the Tathagatas bear witness that the state of self-realisation is free from words and discriminations and has nothing to do with the dualistic way of speaking, that is, all beings receive the teachings of the Tathagatas through self-realisation of Noble Wisdom, not through words of discrimination.

Again, Mahamati, there has always been an eternally-abiding Reality. The "substance" of Truth (dharmadhatu) abides forever whether a Tathagata appears in the world or not. So does the Reason of all things (dharmata) eternally abide; so does Reality (paramartha) abide and keep its order. What has been realised by myself and all other Tathagatas is this Reality (Dharmakaya), the eternally-abiding self-orderliness of Reality; the "suchness" (tat hata) of things; the realness of things (bhutata); Noble Wisdom which is Truth itself. The sun radiates its splendor spontaneously on all alike and with no words of explanation; in like manner do the Tathagatas radiate the Truth of Noble Wisdom with no recourse to words and to all alike. For these reasons is it stated by me that from the night of the Enlightenment to the night of the Tathagata's Parinirvana, he has not uttered, nor ever will he utter, one word. And the same is true of all the Buddhas.

*

THEN SAID MAHAMATI: Blessed One, you speak of the sameness of all the Buddhas, but in other places you have spoken of Dharmata-Buddha, Nishyanda-Buddha and Nirmana-Buddha as though they were different from each other; how can they be the same and yet different?

The Blessed One replied: I speak of the different Buddhas as opposed to the views of the philosophers who base their teachings on the reality of an external world of form and who cherish discriminations and attachments arising therefrom; against the teachings of these philosophers I disclose the Nirmana-Buddha, the Buddha of Transformations. In the many transformations of the Tathagata stage, the Nirmana-Buddha establishes such matters as charity, morality, patience, thoughtfulness, and tranquillisation; by right-knowledge he teaches the true understanding of the maya-like nature of the elements that make up personality and its external world; he teaches the true nature of the mind-system as a whole and in the distinctions of its forms, functions and ways of performance. In a deeper sense, The Nirmana-Buddha symbolises the principles of differentiation and integration by reason of which all component things are distributed, all complexities simplified, all thoughts analysed; at the same time it symbolises the harmonising, unifying power of sympathy and compassion; it removes all obstacles, it harmonises all differences, it brings into perfect Oneness the discordant many. For the emancipation of all beings the Bodhisattvas and Tathagatas assume bodies of transformation and employ many skillful devices, — this is the work of the Nirmana-Buddha.

For the enlightenment of the Bodhisattvas and their sustaining along the stages, the Inconceivable is made realisable. The Nishyanda-Buddha, the "Out-flowing-Buddha," through Transcendental Intelligence, reveals the true meaning and significance of appearances, discrimination, attachment; and of the power of habit-energy which is accumulated by them and conditions them; and of the un-bornness, the emptiness, the egolessness of all things. Because of Transcendental Intelligence and the purification of the evil out-flowings of life, all dualistic views of existence and nonexistence are transcended and by self-realisation of Noble Wisdom the true imagelessness of Reality is made manifest. The inconceivable glory of Buddha-hood is made manifest in rays of Noble Wisdom; Noble Wisdom is the self-nature of the Tathagatas. This is the work of the Nishyanda-Buddha. In a deeper sense, the Nishyanda-Buddha symbolises the emergence of the principles of intellection and compassion but as yet undifferentiated and in perfect balance, potential but unmanifest. Looked at from the in-going side of the Bodhisattvas, Nishyanda-Buddha is seen in the glorified bodies of the Tathagatas; looked at from the forth-going side of Buddhahood, Nishyanda-Buddha is seen in the radiant personalities of the Tathagatas ready and eager to manifest the inherent Love and Wisdom of the Dharmakaya.

Dharmata-Buddha is Buddhahood in its self-nature of Perfect Oneness in whom absolute tranquillity prevails. As Noble Wisdom, Dharmata-Buddha transcends all differentiated knowledge, is the goal of intuitive self-realisation, and is the self-nature of the Tathagatas. As Noble Wisdom, Dharmata-Buddha is inscrutable, ineffable, unconditioned. Dharmata-Buddha is the Ultimate Principle of Reality from which all things derive their being and truthfulness, but which in itself transcends all predicates. Dharmata Buddha is the central sun which holds all, illumines all. Its inconceivable Essence is made manifest in the "out-flowing" glory of Nishyanda-Buddha and in the transformations of Nirmana-Buddha.

*

THEN SAID MAHAMATI: Pray tell us, Blessed One, more about the Dharmakaya?

The Blessed One replied: We have been speaking of it in terms of Buddhahood, but as it is inscrutable and beyond predicate we may just as well speak of it as the Truth-body, or the Truth-principle of Ultimate Reality *(Paramartha)*. This Ultimate Principle of Reality may be considered as it is manifested under seven aspects: First, as *Citta-gocara,* it is the world of spiritual experience and the abode of the Tathagatas on their outgoing mission of emancipation. It is Noble Wisdom manifested as the principle of irradiancy and individuation. Second, as *Jnana,* it is the mind-world and its principle of intellection and consciousness. Third, as *Dristi,* it is the realm of dualism which is the physical world of birth and death wherein are manifested all the differentiations of thinker, thinking and thought-about and wherein are manifested the principles of sensation, perception, discrimination, desire, attachment and suffering.

Fourth, because of the greed, anger, infatuation, suffering and need of the physical world incident to discrimination and attachment, it reveals a world beyond the realm of dualism wherein it appears as the integrating principle of charity and sympathy. Fifth, in a realm still higher, which is the abode of the Bodhisattva stages, and is analogous to the mind-world, where the interests of heart transcend those of the mind, it appears as the principle of compassion and self-giving. Sixth, in the spiritual realm where the Bodhisattvas attain Buddhahood, it appears as the principle of perfect Love *(Karuna).* Here the last clinging to an ego-self is abandoned and the Bodhisattva enters into his self-realisation of Noble Wisdom which is the bliss of the Tathagata's perfect enjoyment of his inmost nature. Seventh, as *Prajna* it is the active aspect of the Ultimate Principle wherein both the forth-going and the in-coming principles are alike implicit and potential, and wherein both Wisdom and Love are in perfect balance, harmony and Oneness.

These are the seven aspects of the Ultimate Principle of Dharmakaya, by reason of which all things are made manifest and perfected and then reintegrated, and all remaining within its inscrutable Oneness, with no signs of individuation, nor beginning, nor succession, nor ending. We speak of it as Dharmakaya, as Ultimate Principle, as Buddhahood, as Nirvana; what matters it? They are only other names for Noble Wisdom.

Mahamati, you and all the Bodhisattva-Mahasattvas should avoid the erroneous reasonings of the philosophers and seek for a self-realisation of Noble Wisdom.

Chapter XIII

NIRVANA

THEN SAID MAHAMATI to the Blessed One: Pray tell us about Nirvana?

The Blessed One replied: The term, Nirvana, is used with many different meanings, by different people, but these people may be divided into four groups: There are people who are suffering, or who are afraid of suffering, and who think of Nirvana; there are the philosophers who try to discriminate Nirvana; there are the class of disciples who think of Nirvana in relation to themselves; and, finally there is the Nirvana of the Buddhas.

Those who are suffering or who fear suffering, think of Nirvana as an escape and a recompense. They imagine that Nirvana consists in the future annihilation of the senses and the sense-minds; they are not aware that Universal Mind and Nirvana are One, and that this life-and-death world and Nirvana are not to be separated. These ignorant ones, instead of meditating on the imagelessness of Nirvana, talk of different ways of emancipation. Being ignorant of, or not understanding, the teachings of the Tathagatas, they cling to the notion of

Nirvana that is outside what is seen of the mind and, thus, go on rolling themselves along with the wheel of life and death.

As to the Nirvanas discriminated by the philosophers: there really are none. Some philosophers conceive Nirvana to be found where the mind-system no more operates owing to the cessation of the elements that make up personality and its world; or is found where there is utter indifference to the objective world and its impermanency. Some conceive Nirvana to be a state where there is no recollection of the past or present, just as when a lamp is extinguished, or when a seed is burnt, or when a fire goes out; because then there is the cessation of all the substrate, which is explained by the philosophers as the non-rising of discrimination. But this is not Nirvana, because Nirvana does not consist in simple annihilation and vacuity.

Again, some philosophers explain deliverance as though it was the mere stopping of discrimination, as when the wind stops blowing, or as when one by self-effort gets rid of the dualistic view of knower and known, or gets rid of the notions of permanency and impermanency; or gets rid of the notions of good and evil; or overcomes passion by means of knowledge;— to them Nirvana is deliverance. Some, seeing in "form" the bearer of pain are alarmed by the notion of "form" and look for happiness in a world of "no-form." Some conceive that in consideration of individuality and generality recognisable in all things inner and outer, that there is no destruction and that all beings maintain their being for ever and, in this eternality, see Nirvana. Others see the eternality of things in the conception of Nirvana as the absorption of the finite-soul in Supreme Atman; or who see all things as a manifestation of the vital-force of some Supreme Spirit to which all return; and some, who are especially silly, declare that there are two primary things, a primary substance and a primary soul, that react differently upon each other and thus produce all things from the transformations of qualities; some think that the world is born of action and interaction and that no other cause is necessary; others think that Ishvara is the free creator of all things; clinging to these foolish notions, there is no awakening, and they consider Nirvana to consist in the fact that there is no awakening.

Some imagine that Nirvana is where self-nature exists in its own right, unhampered by other self-natures, as the varigated feathers of a peacock, or various precious crystals, or the pointedness of a thorn. Some conceive being to be Nirvana, some non-being, while others conceive that all things and Nirvana are not to be distinguished from one another. Some, thinking that time is the creator and that as the rise of the world depends on time, they conceive that Nirvana consists in the recognition of time as Nirvana. Some think that there will be Nirvana when the "twenty-five" truths are generally accepted, or when the king observes the six virtues, and some religionists think that Nirvana is the attainment of paradise.

These views severally advanced by the philosophers with their various reasonings are not in accord with logic nor are they acceptable to the wise. They all conceive Nirvana dualistically and in some causal connection; by these discriminations philosophers imagine Nirvana, but where there is no rising and no disappearing, how can there be discrimination? Each philosopher relying on his own textbook from which he draws his understanding, sins against the truth, because truth is not where he imagines it to be. The only result is that it sets his mind to wandering about and becoming more confused as Nirvana is not to be found by mental searching, and the more his mind becomes confused the more he confuses other people.

As to the notion of Nirvana as held by disciples and masters who still cling to the notion of an ego-self, and who try to find it by going off by themselves into solitude: their notion of Nirvana is an eternity of bliss like the bliss of the Samadhis—for themselves. They recognise that the world is only a manifestation of mind and that all discriminations are of the mind, and so they forsake social relations and practise various spiritual disciplines and in solitude seek self-realisation of Noble Wisdom by self-effort. They follow the stages to the sixth and attain the bliss of the Samadhis, but as they are still clinging to egoism they do not attain the "turning-about" at the deepest seat of consciousness and, therefore, they are not free from the thinking-mind and the accumulation of its habit-energy. Clinging to the bliss of the Samadhis, they pass to their Nirvana, but it is not the Nirvana of the Tathagatas. They are of those who have "entered the stream"; they must return to this world of life and death.

*

THEN SAID MAHAMATI to the Blessed One: When the Bodhisattvas yield up their stock of merit for the emancipation of all beings, they become spiritually one with all animate life; they themselves may be purified, but in others there yet remain unexhausted evil and unmatured karma. Pray tell us, Blessed One, how the Bodhisattvas are given assurance of Nirvana? and what is the Nirvana of the Bodhisattvas?

The Blessed One replied: Mahamati, this assurance is not an assurance of numbers nor logic; it is not the mind that is to be assured but the heart. The Bodhisattva's assurance comes with the unfolding insight that follows passion hindrances cleared away, knowledge hindrance purified, and egolessness clearly perceived and patiently accepted. As the mortal-mind ceases to discriminate, there is no more thirst for life, no more sex-lust, no more thirst for learning, no more thirst for eternal life; with the disappearance of these fourfold thirsts, there is no more accumulation of habit-energy; with no more accumulation of habit-energy the defilements on the face of Universal Mind clear away, and the Bodhisattva attains self-realisation of Noble Wisdom that is the heart's assurance of Nirvana.

There are Bodhisattvas here and in other Buddha-lands, who are sincerely devoted to the Bodhisattva's mission and yet who cannot wholly forget the bliss of the Samadhis and the peace of Nirvana—for themselves. The teaching of Nirvana in which there is no substrate left behind, is revealed according to a hidden meaning for the sake of these disciples who still cling to thoughts of Nirvana for themselves, that they may be inspired to exert themselves in the Bodhisattva's mission of emancipation for all beings. The Transformation-Buddhas teach a doctrine of Nirvana to meet conditions as they find them, and to give encouragement to the timid and selfish. In order to turn their thoughts away from themselves and to encourage them to a deeper compassion and more earnest zeal for others, they are given assurance as to the future by the sustaining power of the Buddhas of Transformation, but not by the Dharmata-Buddha.

The Dharma which establishes the Truth of Noble Wisdom belongs to the realm of the Dharmata-Buddha. To the Bodhisattvas of the seventh and eighth stages, Transcendental Intelligence is revealed by the Dharmata-Buddha and the Path is pointed out to them which they are to follow. In the perfect self-realisation of Noble Wisdom that follows the inconceivable transformation death of the Bodhisattva's individualised will-control, he no longer lives unto himself, but the life that he lives thereafter is the Tathagata's universalised life as manifested in its transformations. In this perfect self-realisation of Noble Wisdom the Bodhisattva realises that for Buddhas there is no Nirvana.

The death of a Buddha, the great Parinirvana, is neither destruction nor death, else would it be birth and continuation. If it were destruction, it would be an effect-producing deed, which it is not. Neither is it a vanishing nor an abandonment, neither is it attainment, nor is it of no attainment; neither is it of one significance nor of no significance, for there is no Nirvana for the Buddhas.

The Tathagata's Nirvana is where it is recognised that there is nothing but what is seen of the mind itself; is where, recognising the nature of the self-mind, one no longer cherishes the dualisms of discrimination; is where there is no more thirst nor grasping; is where there is no more attachment to external things. Nirvana is where the thinking-mind with all its discriminations, attachments, aversions and egoism is forever put away; is where logical measures, as they are seen to be inert, are no longer seized upon; is where even the notion of truth is treated with indifference because of its causing bewilderment; is where, getting rid of the four propositions, there is insight into the abode of Reality. Nirvana is where the twofold passions have subsided and the twofold hindrances are cleared away and the twofold egolessness is patiently accepted; is where, by the attainment of the "turning-about" in the deepest seat of consciousness, self-realisation of Noble Wisdom is fully entered into, — that is the Nirvana of the Tathagatas.

Nirvana is where the Bodhisattva stages are passed one after another; is where the sustaining power of the Buddhas upholds the Bodhisattvas in the bliss of the Samadhis; is where compassion for others transcends all thoughts of self; is where the Tathagata stage is finally realised.

Nirvana is the realm of Dharmata-Buddha; it is where the manifestation of Noble Wisdom that is Buddhahood expresses itself in Perfect Love for all; it is where the manifestation of Perfect Love that is Tathagatahood expresses itself in Noble Wisdom for the enlightenment of all;—there, indeed, is Nirvana!

There are two classes of those who may not enter the Nirvana of the Tathagatas: there are those who have abandoned the Bodhisattva ideals, saying, they are not in conformity with the sutras, the codes of morality, nor with emancipation. Then there are the true Bodhisattvas who, on account of their original vows made for the sake of all beings, saying, "So long as they do not attain Nirvana, I will not attain it myself," voluntarily keep themselves out of Nirvana. But no beings are left outside by the will of the Tathagatas; some day each and every one will be influenced by the wisdom and love of the Tathagatas of Transformation to lay up a stock of merit and ascend the stages. But, if they only realised it, they are already in the Tathagata's Nirvana for, in Noble Wisdom, all things are in Nirvana from the beginning.